MW01705411

# WEB STRATEGY FUNDAMENTALS

Anders Tufvesson

Author Anders Tufvesson 2009

TUK Förlag AB
Östra Kanalgatan 10
652 20 KARLSTAD
Sweden
www.tuk.se
www.webstrategyfundamentals.com

Printed by Lightning Source Inc
Layout Henrik Hedlund, Chaos Media

ISBN 978-91-86419-09-7

# Innehåll

# Foreword

It's a great adventure to write books about issues that change as quickly as the Internet does. What seems true one day can be considered completely passé the next. The latest fad that everyone invests in one week can be left behind the week after. And yet it is more important than ever to place the web, web strategy and the entire company's operation on the net in a larger context. To tell the whole story, not just fragments.

For too long we've settled for fixing a little bit here, changing a little bit there. For too long has the company's work consisted of a patchwork of small efforts, each in itself not bad, but seldom part of a larger plan. The method of trial and error, of not planning big enormous projects is still okay. But it's just as important to look up and to think strategically. This is nothing new. What is new, however, is that the net is now generally accepted. Before, we could manage the net as a digital extension of our usual communication that often started in our shops, with our sales people, in newspaper ads or in TV ads. In the future, these channels will end up further back in the chain. From now on, the net is the starting point for the dialogue with our customers – not as an appendix where visitors occasionally land. This is nothing new either, but for many, it is still quite distant in practice. For many, their web is perhaps not a necessary evil, but a very odd bird. And there are often quite a few who ask questions that haven't been investigated. Is it the marketing department, the sales department, the IT department or maybe the information department that owns it? Should we sell, offer customer service or market new products? Are the CEO's letters important, or is it more important to focus on our sales team?

Today, we know that we need to be able to answer these questions. And we need to have good answers. For most businesses, their web service forms the basis for communicating to the outside world – regardless of whether they've realized it or not. That is where you can tell about what you do, it's where you can convince and argue, and it's where you can help customers that have questions or viewpoints.

Over time, the net creates a whole new dialogue with the customer. The customers are no longer in the hands of a few suppliers, where customers would be happy to receive products or services at all. Now, in the digital economy, the competition is just a click away. And the competition is not the same old group that met for lunch at the Rotary Club or at the clubhouse at the golf course. In the future, your competitors will come from entirely different branches, from all over the world, and are as interested in your customers as you have been.

This book is therefore more important than you realize. And believe me – we need a book like this. Many are tempted to believe that it's only blogs and quick lunch meetings that work in the digital economy. But experience shows that our need for answers to the big questions is only increasing, and for those answers both books and magazines such as Internetworld are excellently suited. Yes, the world is quickly moving forward, but it's when the wind blows hard that it's most important to have something to hold on to. This book is one of those solid points.

But the book isn't just something to hold on to, something to create order in a world that looks slightly chaotic. It's also a call to action. It's not enough to sit and wait for things to be solved on their own.

And it certainly isn't enough to hope that someone else will get things going. It starts with you and your co-workers. He who wants to succeed on the net can of course have help from others, but most importantly he needs to make sure that he understands, learns and gets involved. A lot can be bought from consultants, a lot can be achieved with modern tools. But the mentality, the engagement and the organization that is required can't be bought. It needs to start with you, in your own enterprise. Because if you don't do anything, you can bet that your competitors will.
Get going!

Magnus Höij
Editor-in-chief
Internetworld

create hiarchy in chaos
Ledgability > looking cool

# Thank you!

Can I really write a book? It was a thought that, even in my wildest dreams, I never would have imagined if it hadn't been for my wife Anna. When she wrote her book ideas started to bounce around in my brain. What if I too could write a book? It's thanks to her support and encouragement that this book exists. Thanks Anna!

The other person I'd like to thank is my colleague Henrik Smedberg who encouraged me to write, and arranged the economic requirements. And then you were involved and read all the time, and came with suggestions for improvement. Thank you Henrik!

I also want to thank Tomas Gustavsson and John Johansson at TUK Förlag AB. I have had such wonderful support from you both from the day I showed you a first synopsis and through the entire process. You have read through my manuscript so many times and came with good feedback and encouraging words. You've done a fantastic job.

Additionally, I would like to thank Mia Ohlsson who has been my linguistic support. Without Mia's support and knowledge, the language in the book would have left a lot to be desired.

I also want to thank my two children Sofia and Johan for encouraging me, and all my colleagues at Two who have helped by reading the book and having good comments, especially Johan Aronsson, Victoria Nilsson, Lotta Jansson, Peter Ljunglöf and our chairman Bengt Göran Bengtner. Huge thanks to Olle Olsson for the lovely cover, Julius D'Silva and Erik Jaime who has done many of the pictures in the book, and Sara Hyléen from Tobii for the eye-tracking images. Finally, I would like to thank Andreas Slätt for the comments on the back cover of the book, as well as Magnus Höij for the lovely foreword.

Finally I would like to give a big and warm thank you to Michelle Cryer who has done a fantastic job translating the book into English and John Sören Petterson at Karlstad University who invested in the translation.

There is a gender neutral term *they*!
Making it say 'she' does not make things more inclusive.

# Introduction

The Web Strategy Book is about how a website is built from a visitor's perspective and the business structures that should be present on today's modern websites. It's not about web design, web development or the various trends that regularly show up on the Internet. Instead, it's about the basic commercial principles that all websites should have. Web strategy is based on existing business models, marketing plans, communication plans and digital communication plans. It doesn't matter if the website is for a municipality, a company, a non-profit organization or a sports association. The basic mechanisms for web strategy are applicable to all types of websites.

There are several groups of intended readers for this book: marketing and sales personnel, web designers, advertising representatives and students; in other words, anyone who deals with marketing, sales and the world wide web.

In the long run, a website should attract the right visitors. When a user comes to a website, she should reach the established goals and in some way become a customer according to the website's description of customer. It's easy to see the intention of a website that sells something directly; it's harder to see the intentions when the business happens offline. This book describes how to make visitors into customers, called converting in the world of the web. The book also discusses how to analyze what happens on a website and how a marketing department or webmaster can see what works and what doesn't on their own websites.

Design is important in creating an impression and eliciting a reaction from the visitor. At the same time, design is often based on trends, and is subject to short-lived fads, which is why this book does not deal with design.

With regards to development, publishing tools, html and other technical aspects, there are many valuable books. This book works for all types of tools and programs for building a website.

The Web Strategy Book is divided into four sections: Before you Build a Website, How to Attract Visitors to the Website, How to Take Care of your Visitors and Turn them into Customers, and How to Analyze your Website to Increase the Business Value. As the book's title suggests, the key word is "business value." The book provides answers to how business value can be created on a website. By business value, I mean that the website should be used to create business and/or to save money for the organization. It should be possible to evaluate the business value of a website by doing an expense-income analysis. In the field of web production, the term "Return on Investment" (ROI) is used to show the profitability of web site.

To avoid confusion, the term organization will be used to represent businesses, governing authorities, municipalities, sports associations etc.

Enjoy this time about web strategy and creating a website that gives "Business by web"!

# *Section 1.* Before you Build a Website

How does one build a website? Normally a project starts with a sketch from an advertising firm that follows the graphic profile with Latin text and pictures that will strengthen a brand. Included in this preliminary design are various functions and a navigation bar. The risk with such a preliminary design is that the customer will take it as the final product, without taking into consideration important strategic deliberations. The result can be standstills in the project right from the start. If, for example, there is a navigation included in the proposal, the project group will often get stuck on the text in the navigation. The navigation bar is usually a standard navigation that looks the same regardless of who designs it. It is ubiquitous enough to fit many business organizations, and says nothing about what the organization does, or who is involved. Below is an example of what this type of navigation bar looks like.This particular navigation bar says nothing

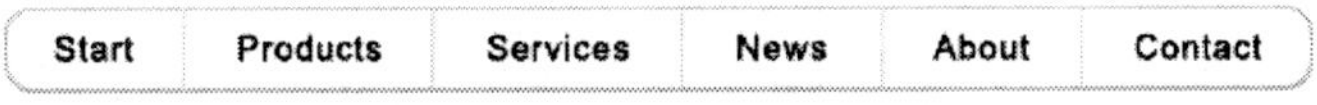


PICTURE 1. Standard navigation

about what the organization does, or to which branch or field of interest they belong. The structure of the navigation is routinely placed in the preliminary proposal without thought or adaptation to the needs

of the website's visitors. Luckily, the number of such projects is declining. Web businesses and customers have gotten better at defining requirements for a website, before the designers and developers begin the actual project.
Before you build a website, a pre-study should be conducted to make sure that the website properly and clearly communicates with the organization's target group(s). An effective pre-study should include the following points:

- the purpose and goals of the website
- the unique selling points of the organization compared to its competitors
- target groups for the website
- "know – feel – do", a model for managing target groups
- goals and how they will be measured
- navigation structure
- analysis of important search words used by visitors
- contents and functions

By using a pre-study, it becomes easier to formulate the requirements for the new website.

## Capture the Needs of the Visitor, not the Internal Organization

When starting to build a new website, the largest obstacle is the organization itself. It is easy to get caught in an "inside-out perspective". It's easy to say that a website should be based on the visitors and their needs and wishes, but it's hard to do. Experience dictates that many web projects go wrong because it's difficult for a project team in an organization to think like an outside visitor. Even with external communication, thoughts and language are often influenced by internal culture. Focus lands on what the organization wants to convey, rather than what the visitor wants. History is rife with examples of people and organizations that think from the inside out.

In the 1970s, Ken Olsen was vice president for Digital Equipment. The company built computers for production and administration. Ken Olsen had apparently said that he saw no reason why someone would want a computer at home. From Ken's perspective, this was common sense, because who would need a computer at home to manage a warehouse?

Ken Olsen had plenty of knowledge about his chosen branch, but still something went wrong. He had access to a large amount of information about his branch and its potential. The opportunity to predict the future was there, but he missed one thing that would have made the prediction much more correct. Olsen lacked the imagination required to see the possibilities outside of his own organization's limits. He saw, quite simply, from the inside out. What the organization delivered could lead to nothing else than to the statement that he made.

The biggest difficulty we meet when building a website is leaving the jargon, the internal language and the internal thought processes in order to see the organization through the eyes of the visitor. Additionally, too many people focus on the technical platform and the problems that follow. In reality, a website project is 90 per cent communication and marketing, and only 10 per cent technical platform. Think about that – 10 per cent technical platform. That means that most of the project will come about in real life, not on the computer. During a website project, imagination must be used to look at the organization with the expectations that the visitor has in mind when she visits the website.

A visitor always has a purpose every time she opens a web browser. It could be to purchase something, to find information or simply to be entertained for a while. There is always an expectation to meet a specific goal. There can also exist a hope to receive a little extra than expected.

## Purpose and General Goals of the Website

The first step in a website project is to think about the purpose and the general goals of the website. Here are some examples of purposes:

- to sell something
- to generate connections with customers
- to improve a brand
- to support and help customers

The website can have one or more of the above stated purposes or maybe another purpose entirely. The purpose of an e-business website is to generate income for the website's owner. The goal is to guide a visitor to buy one (or preferably more than one) product. An e-business website also aims to support existing customers when they have questions and need assistance in using the products they have purchased on or outside the website. If the website sells a complicated product, and the time between the initial interest and the final receipt is drawn out, the website then needs to provide more information than usually exists in a product description. In these cases, the visitor needs more information to be sure that the product is right for her.

### Why is it Important to have the Purpose and Goals Clearly Set Out?

Having the purpose and goals clearly defined explains why the website exists in the first place. It also points to how complicated the website is going to be. There is quite a large difference between building a website for a small business in a small town in North Dakota and creating a global website for a large company active all over the world. The purpose of the small business' website can be to give information to visitors who will visit the actual shop, or to build on the benefits that a brand name can give to the customers. The purpose of the global website is to support the business processes for existing customers, finding new customers and to establish important networking contacts with suppliers and business partners.

The basic thought process must build on what the website will achieve; in other words, what benefits and effects the website will have. Again, this depends on the type of website being discussed and the most important aspect is to see it from the visitor's point of view. The difficulties of this can be explained by the following example. An organization requires a visitor to call a salesperson, but does not take into account that the visitor can visit the website at 7:00pm, when there are no salespeople available. Another example is the customer service-oriented company that has divided their services into "services" and actual "products," where the purpose of the website is to inform visitors about which services are services, and which services have been converted into products. If the visitor is not familiar with the company, there is a risk that she will not find the service she is looking for. She has perhaps chosen the "service" menu in an attempt to find something that the company defines as a "product".

In the dialogues surround the building of a website, the question arises whether the website is designed to sell or to inform. The weight should always lie on the selling side! This applies even to websites that inform. The information should be packaged and "sold" so that the visitor will become interested and take action. A website is not a brochure on the Internet, but a business generator. Business does not always imply that the website needs to actually sell something; it could be that a municipality wants to communicate information prior to educational choices facing students, thereby selling places in the various schools. It could also be that a governmental authority would like for its visitors to use the various e-services on the website to lighten the load of its employees. In other words, they are selling time. The purpose and goals identify what will help the visitors and, in the long run, what will make the website more business-oriented. The purpose and general goals will decide whether a website is needed. Is there a target group that will be interested in the website's contents? Ask the question: "Is there a branch that does not need a website?" The answer is small organizations that sell easily moveable products – products that do not require bulk purchases, for example a small ice cream stand. No one will plan to visit an ice cream stand by searching for "liquorice ice cream Palm Springs" at home and then going to the ice cream stand. On the other hand, the ice cream stand will show up on other websites that the visitor can reach via her mobile phone, and gps-services will search for the nearest ice cream stand that sells liquorice ice cream by the scoop.

The purpose and general goals deal with what we want the visitor to do on our website. When we know that, we can move on to thinking about what it is that makes the organization unique.

## The Unique Selling Points of the Organization Compared to its Competitors

Unique Selling Points (USP) is what separates you from your competitors. It requires figuring out what the company is best at, finding the pros that exist that the competitors do not have. Additionally, the unique points need to be measurable. Common USP's are better service, more knowledgeable staff, better quality and how many years the company has been in business. It is not enough to be unique. Have there been studies done that show that the organization has better service? How can the knowledge of the staff be proven? What is better quality, and how is that measured? There are several methods that can be used to find what is unique. These include SWOT-analysis, Point of difference (POD), Unique perceived benefits (UPB), Kotlers 4 P, or Jack Trouts development of Kotlers 4 P to 5 P. In this book, we use USP as a model, because it is closely related to what visitors demand of a website. Visitors want to know why they should use the organization's products or services; in other words, why the organization is best. Of course, the choice of model depends on what an organization is used to working with. It is entirely possible to choose another model that fits better with the organization.

### Unique Selling Points

A gas station sells gasoline, has a car wash, and sells many other types of products. The quality of the gasoline cannot be a USP, since consumers see gasoline as the same product regardless of supplier. However, "cheapest gasoline" can be a USP, provided that it really is the cheapest. A customer will easily see through a USP that does not add up.

One way of finding one's USP's is to think about why a customer becomes a customer of the organization. A customer questionnaire can, with simple questions, show what the USP's are that may not be clear internally but which are obvious for the customer. The process for finding out USP's includes the following[1]:

- What does the organization do?
- How does the organization do business?
- Who are the organization's customers?
- What do the organization's customers want?
- Why did the customers become customers of the organization?

## What Does the Organization Do?

Make a list of what the organization does and look for things that separate it from its competitors. What is unique? Look for what is special about the products/services/offers. There is often something that can provide a large advantage over the competition, and therefore offers the competitive advantage that an organization needs to beat out one or more of its competitors. It could be an advantage so large that other USP's are unnecessary.

## How Does the Organization do Business?

Is there something different or are there special details that make the organization unique? Delivery within 24 hours, an extra unit of product with orders over 20 pieces, free service, each student receiving a free laptop, or other crucial points in the organization's business concept can all be USP's.

1 The five points are a compilation of various approaches to USP's that are available on various websites. They can naturally be expanded to include other points, but the five listed above provide a guideline over which points are addressed in a USP.

## Who are the Organization's Customers?

What does the organization know about their customer's age, interests, knowledge, activities, gender and other customer-related attributes? Are customer groups spread out over different countries or regions, or are there cultural differences that place different demands on the organization? Perhaps the cheapest does not always work in Beverly Hills. A motorcycle with the best sand protection is a definite sales point in Dubai, but perhaps not in Alaska. "Now available in pink and green" may not be something that will attract a middle-aged businesswoman to buy a mobile phone.

## What do the Organization's Customers Want?

Do the customers want expensive and exclusive, personal service, convenience of access, a good organizational reputation, ease of use or something entirely different? Do different customers have different demands and needs?

List points under each group and try to find out what is it that stands out compared to your competitors. Avoid statements that other organizations can make. Business advantages can provide a designer with an idea of what it is that is unique, thereby providing strategic insights into possible goals for different target groups. Starting with the USP's, try to provide key words to the designer of the website. Words such as flexible, familiar, experience, personal contact, mobility are maybe not unique, but they give the designer a view into the organization's heart and soul. They also provide the web copywriter keywords when text will be written for the website.

## Why did the Customers Become Customers of the Organization?

This is about finding out the reasons a customer is a customer, and why she wants to do business. Sometimes the reasons are unknown to the organization. This is where the possibility arises to identify strengths and perhaps also weaknesses that were not previously visible. As pointed out earlier, these tasks must be approached from an outside-in perspective: the perspective of the customer. Interview customers or do market research and find out why they are customers. Oftentimes reasons appear that can later be used in the marketing process. Other reasons can point to fragile relationships with customers, which would make it easy for the competition to attract customers away from the organization simply by changing their offers and terms slightly.

## The Website's Target Groups

Website target groups are quite different from the target groups referred to in the world of advertising agencies. When a marketing manager is asked what the target group is, the answer comes instantly. The target group could be the 80's generation who have good economy, car dealers, buyers for construction companies, residents of the municipality, or retired women who are interested in reading. If the same marketing manager is asked what the target group of the website is, the answer "everybody" is not unusual, since "everybody" can access the website. The target group that an organization has identified with the help of an advertising agency will give an idea about how the website will communicate with the visitor. It will provide a designer with clues about what the design of the website should look like. If you compare a web site that communicates with several demographic target groups to a web site that focuses on teenagers, the design, structure and contents will most likely be different.

Identifying target groups for a website is more complicated than described above. The same person, in different situations, can belong to different target groups depending on when the website is visited. Let's look, for example, at a car dealership. For a Volvo-retailer, families with children are a target group, but on the website, the same family can end up in different phases/target groups depending on if they are

PICTURE 2. Target groups - who and why

going to buy a new or used car, if they need to repair their car, if they need to buy spare parts and repair it themselves, if they want to change tires, fill up the car with gas, or rent a larger car for a family trip. The same family has different needs. A person who visits a housing manufacturing website could be someone who has built a house before, someone who has never built a house, someone who has bought a house which wasn't complete, or perhaps someone who purchased a "used" house made by the manufacturer.

Different target groups have different needs and wishes about what a website should deliver. One of the challenges for a municipality is to determine the contents and functions that will be sought after by different groups. First and foremost, the residents of the municipality need to have access to relevant information, at the same time that the website can offer valuable services to companies, people interested in moving to the community, tourists and other temporary visitors.

Identifying the target groups that will visit a website and understanding what it is they will want to do is a basic step. If this is not done, there is a large risk that the navigation and structure, contents, purpose and functions are formed based on what the organization thinks the target groups want, not on what is actually demanded by the website's visitors.

## Other Types of Visitors

The next step in the process is to look at the target groups from a perspective that does not have to do with sales. Target groups such as the media, distributors, partner companies, employment seekers and students have other needs than customers. Ask the question "How important are all of these target groups to the organization?" If the organization is active in a field where it is difficult to find competent employees, then job seekers are extremely important. In the long run, it can also be beneficial to have a good relationship with students in colleges and universities. For certain websites, the media is important, for others not. Try to rank the target groups according to how important they are to you, and put your energy into the most important.

Distributors and partner companies often have their own extranet, a special part of the website, where the target groups can log in and access special content.

Another step in working with target groups is the need to differentiate between new and returning visitors. Think about whether the contents of the website look different for the different groups. A new visitor wants basic information about what the website offers and who offers it, while a returning customer will go directly to what is being offered. A returning customer is more likely to be further along in her thinking process, and closer to making a purchase. For larger websites, it can be an option to have different homepages depending on if the visitor is new or returning.

Visitors with varying pre-knowledge are also likely to have different needs, which is important to keep in mind for organizations who sell complicated products, such as houses, swimming pools, or home stereo systems. The length of the process also varies from the moment the need arises to when a product is purchased. In these cases, there needs to be different sections on the website that cater to the varying needs. This can be resolved by having various guides or other functions that help customers. It is a case of educating the visitor, step-by-step. In this way, she is successively provided with information that leads to the desired behaviour.

## Statistics and Web Analysis

In those cases where an organization has an existing website that will be replaced by a new one, the statistics tools from the old website can act as a source of important information. One can see what content and which pages were most viewed, and which key words were used in search engines to find the website. With the help of a web analyst, a lot of information can be extracted from the stats tools about the visitors' intentions. Another source of information is your own website's search function. If you can figure out what words the visitor searched for without finding any hits, then those words are important from a content point of view. Perhaps there will be new pages containing those words on the new website?

## "Know – Feel – Do" or Personas

In certain cases where it can be hard to identify the target groups, there are various techniques or processes that give some structure to the process. These are Know – Feel – Do (KFD) and Personas[2]. If there is any uncertainty as to what target groups are out there, Personas is the best choice. If the target groups are somewhat clearer, then KFD is the way to go. In certain instances, the project might start with Personas, then move on to a KFD analysis.

### Personas

Personas are descriptions of how the different target groups can create individuals with personal characteristics. Start by interviewing people in the organization that have contact with customers. Then interview the customers and try to collect as much information as possible about their needs and wishes from a web perspective. The level of ambition is obviously limited by the available budget. It is possible to obtain relevant material even with a small budget. It's all about limiting the number of interviews in a statistically safe and relevant way. General trends can be observed, even if it's not practical to investigate in the detailed way provided by a larger budget.

The next step is to identify patterns of behaviour evident in the gathered information. Watch for consistent actions, needs and wishes that can be grouped together based on different patterns.

Study the groups and try to chisel out different personalities. Individuals with the same characteristics become a Persona. Try to limit the number of Personas to between five and ten. This number obviously varies depending on the operation and the scope of the website.

2 The KFD model and Personas are taken from various sources on the Internet

## Describe the Personas

Now comes the task of describing the Personas that have been identified. Give them names, ages, needs and goals they want to achieve on the website. Don't forget to describe their contact with the organization. A Persona is described in story-telling format. It is important, though, to keep to the facts that exist in the collected material.

If there are many Personas, try to rank them in order of importance to the organization. The description of the Personas can be divided into the following 4 suggested steps:

- Who is it, and what does she do?
- What is her roll in relationship to the website?
- What does she need from the contents?
- What are her intentions in visiting the website?

## Example of a Persona for a Car Dealership

**Ann Johnson, 37 years old, single mom**

Ann works as a consultant, and drives a used car that is a few years old. Ann doesn't buy new cars; she prefers cars that are two to three years old, and rarely keeps them longer than four years before she trades them in. She likes vehicles with a high safety rating, are environmentally friendly, and with room for her family of three when they go on vacation.

Ann uses the website to book tune ups, because she doesn't know anything about cars, and always uses the garage to repair and service her car. Her work day is busy, and after work, the children take up most of her time, which makes booking a time for car service easier in the evenings via the website. Ann and her children try to take a ski trip once a year. On these occasions, Ann uses the website to find a rental car, since her car does not have room for Ann's parents who follow along on the trip. When Ann is ready to trade in her car, she looks at the used car section on the website, and would prefer to book a test drive, so that she knows that the car will be there to test at a specific time.

Ann's goals:

- book service and repairs
- rent a larger car
- find a car and book a test drive.

## Know – Feel – Do

In those cases where the organization has a fairly good idea of the relevant target groups, the technique "Know – Feel – Do" can be of use. This is where we find out what the target groups will know, feel and do when they visit the website.

### Know

What do you want the visitor to know or learn during their visit to the website? Be clear about what the target group needs when they visit, and identify what they need to know to be able to make some kind of decision. In the know-phase, it's also good to know where the customer stands: is she far from making a purchase, or is she fairly certain about what she wants? Depending on where the visitor is in that process, the know-knowledge probably is going to be different.

### Feel

How should the visitor feel when she visits the website? The combination of contents, function and design will bring forth this feeling. Try to think in terms of "confident in their decision", "happy", "must-have-feeling." Confidence in having made the right decision, happy about receiving a product, or the feeling of wanting to have a product or service. Everything can be achieved by the website's contents, functions and design[3].

## Do

What do you want the visitor to do on the website? Which of the organization's goals will the visitor contribute to? This is all about very concrete actions, such as sending in a request for information, book a time for a test drive, contact a salesperson, buy something or other things that the website can deliver.

## Other Ways to Work with Target Groups

Another way to find the right target groups is to work with focus groups – groups of visitors from the different target groups. With the help of questions and direction, the focus groups give an idea of their needs. The downside of focus groups is that humans are by nature pack animals. We will go along with others, and in a group of different types of people, there is a risk that not everyone will say what they think, because others "seem to know what they're talking about" or take up too much space. From a target group perspective, individual interviews are a better course of action. If there is time and money, focus groups can be a nice complement. When creating new ideas and functions on a website, focus groups can be the way to go. Focus groups offer the possibility of brainstorming. Developments happen by group members expanding on each other's ideas. Focus groups give dynamism, and allow individuals to interact, thereby coming upon new solutions to problems.

---

3 As mentioned before, this is not a book about design, which is why we're not giving any design examples. The feel-phase acts a base for the designer, and will help the designer with how the website should look.

## Measureable Goals that can be Followed Up

We talked earlier about the purpose and general goals of the website. The examples we gave were:

- to sell something
- to generate interest among customers
- to improve a brand
- to support and help customers

Now it's time to find the measureable goals for the website. Measureable goals, or "Key Performance Indicators" (KPI), are the metrics that need to be on a website so we can decide if the website is profitable. It is important that the website gives a return on the investment made, called "Return on Investment" (ROI). The income generated needs to surpass the cost of the website, so that the website creates a profit for the organization. Otherwise the website will be seen as simply a cost. If there is a good revenue model that shows where the organization makes its profit from the website, then it becomes infinitely easier to invest both time and money later on. There are many measureable goals. Here are a few:

- an order, a reservation, a purchase
- a subscription to a newsletter
- a request for more information
- a download of a pdf or other document
- contact with someone
- a certain number of pages visited
- the amount of time the visitor spends on the website
- x percent of traffic generated by search engines
- the number of unique visitors over a period of time

Ideally, whether the website's goals are being met or not should be easily calculated by statistical tools and/or by using other metric functions. There are some goals that are more difficult to measure using these tools, for example "to improve a brand." Despite the measurement problems, it may be so that a targeted and user-friendly website is the best way to improve a brand. We want a website that improves and generates business, not an expensive brochure on the Internet that simply conveys the same information as other marketing campaigns.

## Measuring Visits and Visitors

The most common measuring value used on today's websites is the number of visitors. This is often a number that is measured and then displayed by an organization:

- We have 1 000 visitors every day
- We have 100 000 visits each month
- We have 2 000 unique visitors each month

These are three very different statements with three very different implications. The first one is 1 000 visitors per day, which includes both new and returning visitors, of which 40 could actually be unique visitors that return to the website often.

The second statement is not about visitors, but about visits, and presents the same problem as the first statement. We don't know how many of those visits are new unique customers, we only know how many times the website is visited. We don't know how many visitors have generated this amount of visits.

The third statement clearly deals with the number of unique visitors. In other words, there are 2 000 unique web browsers. A unique visitor is, in other words, a unique web browser on a computer. If someone were to visit a website from the same computer, but use two different web browsers, the website counts that as two unique visitors. If several people have access the same computer, they are counted as the same visitor (i.e. web browser). As long as the website doesn't require logging in, unique visitors is the best measure we have for measuring visitors on websites.

It is interesting to keep track of unique visitors over time – to monitor the traffic and see if it decreases or increases from one month to another. Other points of interest with unique visitors are variations over a weeklong period, or if there are seasonal variations. However, taken out of context, this is a fairly worthless measurement. Ask yourself the question: "Is ten visitors or a hundred thousand visitors better?" The answer is: "It depends on what they do." Do the visitors achieve the goals of the website or not? If seven of those ten accomplish one or more goals, then the challenge is to increase the number of visitors. If only one of the hundred thousand visitors does what we want, the challenge then becomes making the website easier to use. A prerequisite is, of course, that we reach the right target group. Study the web statistics, and try to see where the users get lost, where do they get stuck in trying to achieve their goal. In chapter four of this book, we will go into more detail about how follow-ups, analysis and statistics work.

## Finding KPI's and Making them Measureable

Using the purpose and goals of the website, it's time to outline the KPI's , the measureable goals of the website. Different websites fulfil different needs. An e-business website wants a visitor to make a decision to buy something in the easiest possible way. Another goal is to have a visitor buy more, using suggestive selling: "People who bought this also bought the following products" (shown in the vicinity of the product the customer is looking at). Every website can have at least two to three KPI's. Through statistical tools and other measuring tools, the goals should be checked on a regular basis. One way to do this is to use a meter that shows red, yellow or green, or in some other way illustrates the results like a traffic light, where red is bad and green is good. If the results show yellow or red, it's time to look at the results more closely to find the problem. The frequency of the monitoring depends on the KPI being measured. An example is Amazon.com that uses a warning system to signal when their most important KPI's are falling below critical points. Other websites have weekly or monthly reporting to the key people in the organization.

The follow-ups' frequency should be based on how much money the organization is prepared to lose. This is something that is very individual for each organization, and it can take a while before a reasonable amount is agreed upon. The decision on whether the follow-ups should be done monthly, weekly, daily, or several times a day is related to the possible loss the organization incurs during the same time period if they don't follow up and analyze the statistics.

## Navigation Structures

Navigation on a website is the most important interface for making sure the visitor can find the content she wants. A good navigation structure helps a visitor, a bad one hinders. Everyone who has used the Internet as a tool has been trained to think that the visitor must reach her information in three clicks. **This is no longer valid.** The new truth is that as long as the trail is "hot," the visitor can click as many times as she wants, and as soon as the trail goes cold, she goes back to the search engine to investigate the next link. This means that we can lose a visitor before she has even clicked once, but we can also keep her clicking on the website several times. A navigation structure that works and is geared towards the target group creates the proper circumstances for the latter. The prerequisite is that the visit starts well, and the visitor feels that she has come to the right place.
A poor navigation system is one that doesn't describe the website's contents to the visitor. This is not good, since there is not much time before the visitor decides whether she will stay or not. The following example of a poor navigation bar doesn't help the customer out very much.

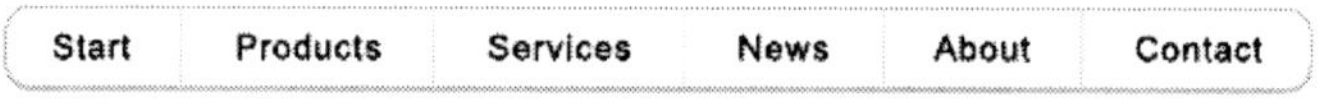


PICTURE 3. Example of a navigation that doesn't support a visitor

This type of top navigation doesn't tell the visitor what the organization does. It's entirely neutral, and could fit any number of different organizations. In most cases, this type of navigation is wrong. It doesn't take care of the needs that exist from a visitor's perspective. Its existence can be justified for an organization that sells physical products and the associated services.

Top navigation can, in those cases, be complemented by a variation of target group portals placed near the navigation bar. For example:

PICTURE 4. Example of a standard navigation complemented by target group portals

Here, the navigation is complemented by five target group portals that each lead to a different start page with appropriate contents.

## Target Group-based Navigation

A target group-based navigation starts with the needs of the target groups. Car dealerships have an operation that, in most cases, is ideal for target group-based navigation:

PICTURE 5. Example of a slightly sparse car dealership navigation

Let's pretend that someone has been out to the mall to shop. When she comes out to her car, she finds a large dent and significant paint scratch on the front door, with no note on the windshield. It's after 6pm, and the car dealership is closed. Where do you think this person will click to see if the dealership has a paint workshop? Where will she click if she also wants to find out if she can rent a car while the car is being repaired? The problem with this navigation is that there is no link that will help the visitor. Via "service," the visitor finds a simple form to fill in to book a time for service. Most will then choose "other services" and there they will find:

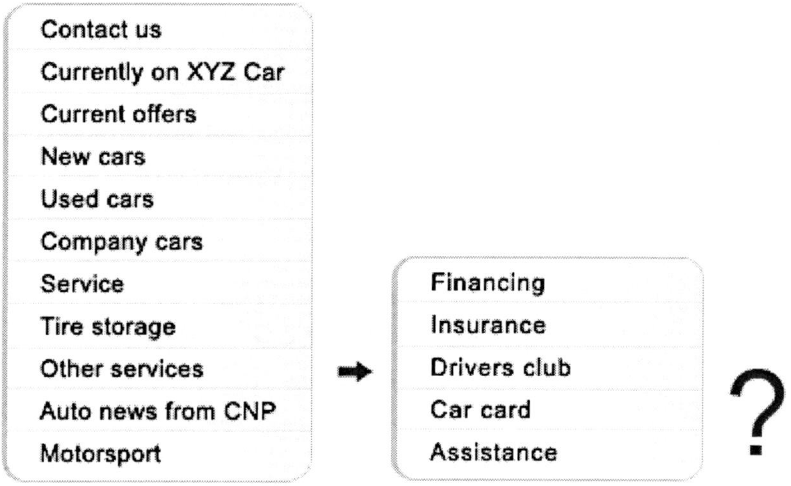


PICTURE 6. Sub-menu for "Other services"

With the navigation, the visitor couldn't find anything thing she was looking for. The navigation is disrupted because the dealership wants to be both local and global, and to reach specific target groups. The company has paid tire storage, and passes on news from something called CNP. Plus, they differentiate between new, used and company cars. It really is just sales organizations that make the difference between a new car and a company car, yet they use very different navigation entries. Compare with the following top navigation bar:

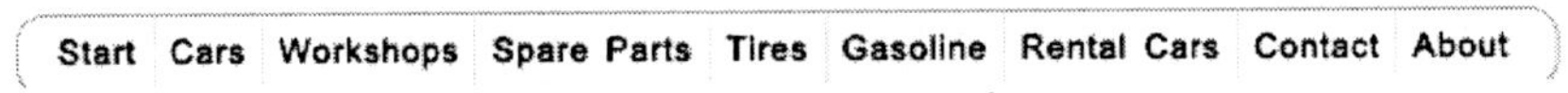


PICTURE 7. Car buyer navigation adjusted for target groups

This is a clear top navigation bar that organizes the web page according to car ownership over time. The first thing a customer can do is to read about cars. It doesn't matter if it's new or used, if it's for private or company use. This is followed by all the services offered, such as garage, spare parts, tires, etc. It is worth it to note that the top navigation structure doesn't follow the structure of the organization. If there is anything that is certain about the organization it's that there will be changes in its structure. The choice of words in the navigation bar is based on customer needs, however, which is something that will not change over time.

Additionally, there are certain words that are inappropriate from an inside-out perspective. Presumably the company doesn't just sell gasoline, but also diesel, ethanol, and maybe biogas or CNG's. However, a visitor will say gas, or maybe gas station. There is no doubt either about what type of company the website is, or what they offer in terms of services. The visitor understands this through the language of the navigation bar.

## Supply-based Navigation

A supply-based navigation is also based on target groups, although not quite in the same way as the car example above. Consideration is also given to what it is that's offered.

PICTURE 8. Example of supply-based navigation

Someone wants to visit the racetrack, and chooses "Visit the racetrack." At the same time, she is new to the racetrack, and therefore can find information under "For Beginners". If she then wants to know more about horse racing, and how to place bets, she can choose "Sports and Betting." In addition, there are other portals for other important target groups, for example conference and event organisers who would click on "Conference and Arena." The navigation bar is clear, and a visitor will more than likely find what it is she came to the website to do or read. The visitor also understands what kind of website she has landed on, since the navigation bar includes words that are specific to the field.

### Product or Service-based Navigation

In product or service-based navigation, it's the products and services that are in focus.

PICTURE 9. Example of product-based navigation

In the above example, the products dictate the navigation tool. It's easy to find what's supplied, and there should be no doubt for the visitor about where to look to find what she wants. It is also clear what the website does.

## Dual Navigation

One way to make top navigation clearer is to divide the bar into two rows. We're not talking about two separate rows, but a clear navigating system with a choice in each field.

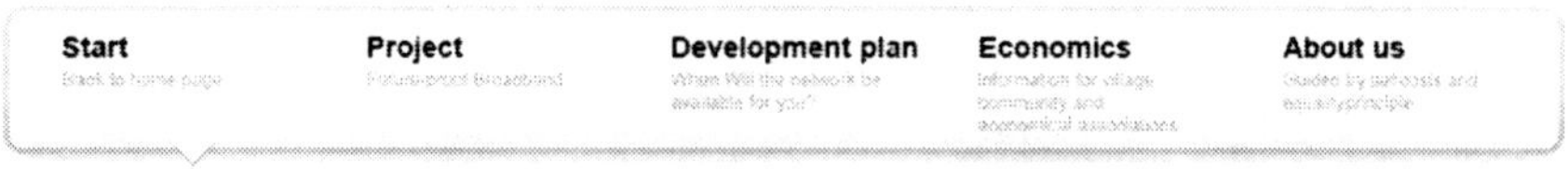


PICTURE 10. Example of dual navigation

The first row is the name of the tab, the second row is a description of what the tab contains. This type of navigation can be used when it is difficult to find the right words in the navigation bar, and another line of explanation can make the choices clearer.

## lContent can Help Find the Right Navigation Tool

Content and function is the next point to address when building a website. Part of the reason why I go through top navigation first before we even think about content is to see what navigation should look like, and then to challenge that with the content. When top navigation, contents and functions are all in the right place, it becomes much easier to make sure that the structure is appropriate. Write the proposed top navigation on a piece of paper. Let five to ten people answer approx. ten questions about where they would click to find a certain type of content. In this way, it's quite easy to find out where the faults are in the navigation. If you have more then 10-20 percent of wrong answers, then there is probably something wrong. Rework the navigation bar, and repeat the procedure with new people. Note that is it good if these people belong to the target groups, but it's not entirely necessary. If there are 5-10 percent wrong answers, look at the types of wrong answers that showed up. In certain instances, the contents can be poorly placed; in other cases it could be that the chosen language in the navigation bar is not accurate. Repeat the procedure again if you like, with a new group of people, just to make sure that there are no other faults.

## The Number of Choices in the Top Navigation Bar

Websites are getting wider in terms of pixels[4]in relation to larger screens becoming available. There are still limits to how wide a website can be without it coming across as too large and sprawling. The same thing applies to the top navigation bar. If there are too many choices, it becomes troublesome. Of course, everything depends on the design,

4 According to Wikipedia, a pixel, or picture element, is the smallest unit of a graphic image that can be controlled. A computer screen resolution can be set to, for example, 1024x768, which means 1024 horizontal pixels and 768 vertical pixels.

but guidelines suggest having between six and nine choices. Any more and it becomes difficult for the visitor to find what she wants. There are exceptions, and websites with more choices are starting to pop up. It is a development that risks complicating things for the visitor. In those cases, it's better to find other ways to divide the website into different sections, or perhaps divide the content into different websites, for example one website for the organization, and one website for the organization's online shop.

When the top navigation is in place, and the contents have been placed, it's just as important that the lower levels' content is grouped properly. Appropriate menu words and ranking is very important here as well. The navigation should feel balanced and be placed in such an order that the visitor finds it logical and easy to follow. A well-thought-out navigation structure produces a website that is easy to use, and also makes it easier for the web editor to maintain existing and add new content.

# Keyword Analysis

Electric power interruption, rescue services, recycling plant, revised tax deductions, and child welfare are commonplace words and phrases for certain organizations. Normal people, however, will say power outage, fire department, dump, adjustments and day care. Again, we're looking at an inside-out perspective. What an organization thinks a visitor will search for in a search engine is not always accurate. The language that is used on the website is oftentimes the language that is used within the organization. IT-language is full of TLA's – Three-Letter-Abbreviations, most of which are incomprehensible to people from the outside. Municipalities and government bodies have proper bureaucratic terms for many of the services they offer to the public. Auditing offices have economic terms that make laymen's skin crawl. There are examples of words from every branch and organization that are used within the field, but not by the target groups. To ensure that the texts on a website are written at the right level, and that the website ranks high (is among the top hits in the search engine result list), a keyword analysis should always be done. Keywords and phrases describe what a website is all about.

When a new website is being built, it's important to keep the following in mind. In order for individual pages from a new website to rank well in search engine results, it is fundamental that the pages support appropriately chosen keywords or phrases. The trend is to have more words in the same search. With more words, it's often easier to find the content you're looking for, since the competition on the results pages has gotten stiff, and the searcher wants a search result that is as relevant as possible. The trend also points to users typing in entire sentences in the search engine, and that they are sometimes questions. In this case, the search engine will look for a page that contains the actual question – not the answer that the searcher was hoping for.

This is why it's good to have normal questions and answers on the organization's website. To be able to rank keywords (the generic term keywords will apply whether it is one word or several), there needs to be at least one page that focuses on that keyword.

There is another trend in searching which show that we don't just search for "painter" but for "painter New Jersey wallpapering." We've become used to using search engines, and therefore become more specific in our searches. The local aspect is being noticed more and more, especially in searches where the business takes place, not over the web, but locally in an actual store. We specify the search to what we want done, or what we want to do.

To do a keyword analysis, the organization needs to think about what words their target groups will search for to reach a website. If you are not already at the top of the search engine's list with your organization's name or your brand, then these need to be part of the analysis. Remember that the people who will search for the organization's name already know about you and what you do. With general keywords, you become accessible to people who don't know about you.

Do try to avoid so-called generic keywords, though – the ones that can mean several things. An example of a generic keyword is "to burn." Someone can burn a CD, burn themselves on the iron, be burned by fireworks or burn money. This makes such words difficult to rank highly in a search engine's results. This is especially true when the word is used in a way that is more common than the usage employed by the organization. A list of keywords should contain twenty to forty words or phrases. In those instances where a generic word is important to an organization, then it should naturally be used in texts on the website, but it will likely not rank very high in a search engine.

## Analyzing Keywords

There are many tools on the web to analyze keywords. Google has a number of different tools, where you can analyze how many people search for a given keyword per month, and the number of searches in the last month. They also have trend analysis – how keyword searches change over time. Google's keyword tool also has a synonym tool, which will suggest other words that are searched for in conjunction to the word being looked at. Google provides information on which words are searched for most, and which are not as common.

There are other useful tools available for examining keywords in English. Aside from Google, you can use Wordtracker.com. Wordtracker is a good alternative to Google, and provides lots of support for keyword analysis. Keyword competition is quite stiff in English, as well, compared to languages like Swedish or Portuguese. This makes it even more important to go with phrases, rather than single keywords. Google and other search engines are constantly developing and improving services so that visitors will have relevant search results, such as related searches. Related searches are suggestions of other searches that are very close to the completed search. For the search word "excavator," related words can be "used excavators" or "Volvo excavators."

Remember that the analysis is used to find common keywords, which will allow for high positioning. Of course, other pages can and should be created for the website. Not every page of a website has to rank high in a search engine. The keywords that are chosen are the ones that will be used for monthly monitoring, to see how well the words rank – where the words land in various search engine result lists. Feel free to compare your results against your competitors'.

Competition is just as important as monitoring how often keywords are searched. In Google's keyword tool, there is a column that shows how stiff the competition is in Google's paid advertising. That number, or rather diagram, gives a hint of the exposure a word has to competition. That information should then be compared with a Google search of the word in question, to see where the competition stands in terms of number of results shown. It's also important to look at the first ten websites that show up, and to decide if your own website can compete using the chosen keyword. For example, it could be tough to position a new website with a new domain name, when the competition has well-established (old) domains and pages that are well prepared. It takes knowledge and experience to be able to judge your competition. If the organization doesn't have that knowledge, bringing in outside help can save both time and money.

## Using Keywords

There are two ways to use the chosen keywords. The first is to write at least one good page for each keyword according to the rules used by different search engines. What these rules are changes almost daily, and are difficult to deal with in a book. Further on, in chapter two, we will deal with the basics of optimizing a search engine – techniques for ensuring a high keyword ranking in the search engines results.

The other way to use keywords is to look at the top navigation bar and try to place the keywords under the right heading. Again, this is about challenging the navigation, and seeing if it can withstand the challenge. If you can't place all the keywords into the navigation, then perhaps there is a misnamed or missing heading. At this point, a decision needs to be made to either rework the navigation bar, put the word aside for a while, or simply remove the word entirely from the list of chosen keywords.

## Keywords as Carewords

Using an organization's keywords shouldn't just be limited to the website – they can also be used on the organization's other communication channels. In this respect, the term "keyword" can be quite limiting. A better term would be "careword". Wider recognition can be achieved if carewords are used consistently across all communication, which works well as leverage since the target groups can identify with the carewords.

When communication is built on words that the target groups themselves use to find an organization, product or service, then it is more than likely that the words are relevant even in advertising, PR, and other marketing strategies. It's all about finding the right words and using them before you competition does.

## Content and Functions

Depending on the publishing tool[5] you use, there is a difference between content and functions. Some tools can manage quite a lot, and the need for developing functions is small, while other publishing tools require you to develop functions. The first step is to identify contents without worrying about function. Write down the content – what the website is going to be filled with. Then look at the different publishing tools, and see what can and can't be done.

The first thing to do with the content of the website is to develop a content strategy. What type of content will there be, and where in the structure will it be easiest to create new content? Today's search engines love new content. Many websites haven't planned or created a strategy for where new content will be posted. News is the most common type of content and, for most organizations, the easiest type of content to create. Still, some organizations have a hard time finding content that can be counted as news, and must therefore find other ways to place new content. References are an example of this. The range of products may be quite static (that is to say, new products or

5 A publishing tool is a tool used for managing and publishing contents on a website. Publishing tool is also known as "Content Management Systems".

services are not continuously added). Hopefully, though, the products that are offered are sold to more and more customers. In this case, a properly reference bank is a good place for new content. Other ways to publish new content is to claim territory in your branch by writing articles about the branch, without promoting your own products or services. Such articles, written by knowledgeable people, are good for both visitors and search engines. Another way is to create a blog on the website. A blog is less pretentious than news, and is a great way to create new content.

When the content is planned with the navigation structure in mind, it will become clear if the website is leaning in one direction or another. What I mean is that certain menu choices in the navigation have much more content than others. It could be time to challenge the navigation again. If there's not enough content, then both menus and searches needs to be re-evaluated to find the optimal structure.

## Summary of Chapter 1

It is easier said than done to think like a visitor. But, the organization is creating a website for the visitor's sake. That's why the basic demands are the most important when creating a successful website. Who is part of the target group, and what do they want to achieve with a visit? This is the most important question when a website is created, or when an existing website gets a makeover. It's about finding out as much about the target group as possible, how they want to use the website, and what information they expect to find. Knowledge of the organization, in addition to the needs of actual visitors, is an important factor for finding these things out. The most dangerous thing to do in the preparation phase is to create a website that only satisfies the internal needs of the organization without listening to the needs of the visitors. Today's visitor also demands an easy-to-use website that communicates clearly. If the website doesn't do this, then there are other websites to visit. With the help of search engines, it becomes easier to find the competitions' websites.

It is also important that a website can be monitored and followed up on, to ensure that the established goals are being met, and to see if a website is profitable or not. All types of organizations have one or more goals they want to achieve with their website, and these goals have to be measureable.

A good and clear website will improve a brand; a bad website can damage it.

# *Section 2.* Attract Visitors to the Website

Attracting visitors is the first step in long-term Internet marketing strategy. The second step is to take care of the visitor and make her into a customer. Today, the most common word used to describe this process of creating customers from visitors is "converting," a word that will be used throughout the rest of this book. The last step is to analyze through web statistics what happens on the website, why it happens, and how it can be made better.

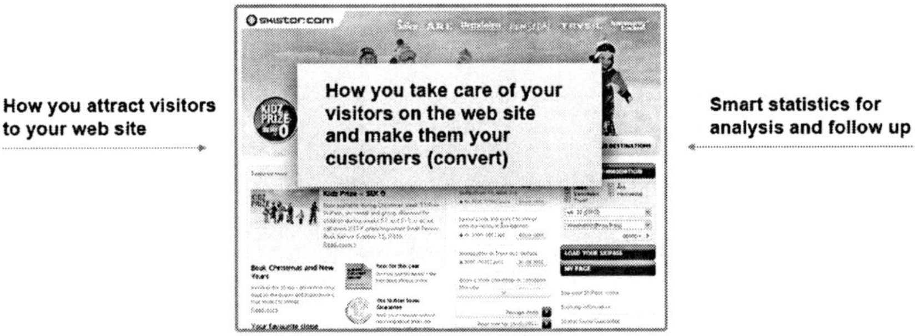


PICTURE 11. Long-term marketing

The most important thing for a website is to attract the right visitor – a visitor that has the desire and the opportunity to achieve the goals set up for the website. How well this process works can be seen with the help of web analysis, i.e. analysis of the statistics generated by the website's statistics tool or other types of measuring systems. This shows whether the website is generating business value for the owner organization. We'll talk more about web analysis in chapter four.

## How to attract visitors

Traditional marketing such as print ads, TV or radio still generate a lot of web traffic. With the Internet, many organizations are using newsletters and other types of web-based marketing such as banners, sponsored links, search engines etc. With this comes viral marketing (from one person to another), where people use word-of-mouth and social networks[8] to tip others about a website or product. Viral marketing increases when people have opportunities to reach out with their tips. In the past, we relied on friends and family for advice. Today, there are many more sources of information on the web, which affect whether a trademark will be improved or stifled.

A 2006 study paints a picture that is still applicable today. It's likely that the percentages have changed somewhat, but the study shows what is important when it comes to getting visitors to come to the website. The study asked the question "How do you find a website that you didn't know about before?" Respondents were allowed to answer with more than one of the given alternatives. The results were the following:

- 71% search engine
- 46% link from another website
- 41% "heard from a friend"
- 38% e-mail from a friend or family member

8 Social networks are online meeting places where individuals discuss various topics through discussion forums, chats, or other web-based tools. Other words for social networks are communities, or Internet meeting areas.

- 29% TV ad
- 28% print ad
- 22% e-mail ad
- 14% radio ad
- 14% keyword marketing
- 9% banner ads
- 5% blogs.

Source: Forrester Group "European Internet Users" 2006.

An educated guess would predict that the percentages for search engines and tips from others have increased. We use search engines more often today than in 2006, and the trend is only increasing. More and more people are also engaging in social media and other websites where products and services are discussed and reviewed. These days, we share more information with each other than ever before. That part of the study is quite exciting. We are becoming more and more social on the web. Our willingness to share and comment on products and brand names is becoming clear, not just between companies that sell products to consumers (business-to-customer or B2C), but also between companies dealing with other companies (business-to-business, or B2B). This trend brings with it a demand that the brand name has a customer-to-customer (C2C) strategy. A C2C-strategy deals with what one customer will say to another customer. In other words, it's about being keeping an eye on the social aspects of the web to see what customers are saying about a brand name. The strategy has to give guidelines on how the organization will deal with negative (or positive) things that show up.

Another emerging trend over the last couple of years is that as soon as an ad is shown on TV, the number of searches for the words and products in the ad increases according to a study from Jupiter Research[9]. People don't necessarily search for the brand name, or the company behind the ad, but for the general words used in the ad. The study also showed that 23 percent of the people who started searching after having seen the ad made a purchase. The corresponding numbers for those who had seen an ad in a newspaper or magazine was 30 percent, and for those who had heard an ad on the radio was 22 percent. There are two outcomes when searches are performed. Searchers either find your website, or your competitor's. How much of the money for your TV-ad will go straight to your competitors?

An example of this is a film ad about a digital camera from a certain manufacturer. After the ad is shown, searches for digital cameras and other words from the ad increase. The ad creates searches, and searches create business. It's important that the creator of the ad is a part of the searches, i.e. the creator should be fighting for the top positions in the search engine results based on the words used in the ad. An alternative is to buy sponsored links. Otherwise there is a large risk that an expensive ad campaign will place the visitors with the competitors. This means that there should always be a strategy to take care of the target groups when they go to the Internet after a traditional media campaign. It's probably not just in relation to TV ads that customers can be lost to the competition; it happens with radio and print ads as well. When a listener is in front of her computer, she may not remember who it was that sent the ad, so she starts searching for what she does remember. There are no concrete studies or other scientific support for this, but the trend is clear: we search more and more on the web for products and information about products.

---

9 Jupiter Research: iProspect Offline Channel Influence on Online Search Behaviour Study (August 2007)

## Different Ways to Attract Visitors to the Website

There are many ways to attract visitors to a website. Most of them are well known, and have been around for years. A traditional way is to use banners that show up on some kind of website and lands on a campaign website. Banner ads and campaign websites are the types of Internet-based ads that are closest to other types of ads (ex. blurbs) and it's easy to integrate a banner campaign into larger campaigns outside the Internet. It's therefore easier for advertising agencies, who are pros at using traditional advertising, to use this type of Internet-based advertising.

Other, more traditional ways are newsletters and sponsored links in a search engine or in social media. All of these are paid advertising, and work as long as an organization is willing to pay for each visit via click cost or another type of payment model.

### Sökmotorer

One of the most effective ways to have relevant visitors is to have the website positioned high in search engines' results lists. Searches in search engines are the most common Internet activity today, including e-mail and chats. We actively search for advertising when we have a need. Ines Uusmann[10] once said that "the Internet is a fad that might just whiz by. I don't think that people have the time that is needed to actually surf the web"[11]. She was entirely correct. A normal user doesn't use the Internet in the same way today as in 1996, when Uusmann made her statement. Then, plenty of people sat and "surfed the net" simply because they could, not because they had a concrete

10 Ines Uusmann was the Swedish Minister of Communication at the time.

11 It is difficult to know exactly what Ines Uusmann said, since there are many sources and explanations as to what she said and how. This is an attempt to provide the general gist of what she said based on the different variations.

purpose. Today, we're extremely goal-oriented when we open a web browser. There is a goal, a desire to find specific information. It could be to buy something, to find information or simply to be entertained for a while. There is always a need. Using the web has become a part of every day life. In 1996, the Internet was new and those that used it were more curious about what they could find than how they could effectively use the Internet for personal and professional purposes. In retrospect, we can give Usmann a little credit. We don't have the time needed to wander around the Internet willy-nilly; we're entirely too focused for that, at least if we look at it from a business perspective.

When a visitor wants to quickly find a website, and doesn't know the address, it's even more important for the organization to be found using the important search words or keywords. The search itself will naturally evolve over time, and it's important that pictures, videos, sound and other formats other than text can be ranked as well. That's why an organization needs to look over their entire digital content, and create pictures, video and audio files that can be indexed, or made available to search engines. There is a risk that pictures could be placed in a catalogue that is not accessible to search engines. Being included in search engines' rankings is also a long-term investment, compared to, say, banner ads, which are more campaign-oriented, and are only visible for a certain period of time.

## Search Engine Optimization

Search engine optimization is actually an incorrect term. It's not the search engine that is optimized, but the pages from the website that are based on chosen keywords and key phrases. The web pages will hopefully rank high in the results page generated by the search engine. A better term would be search word optimization or key word optimization. Optimization happens by choosing whether you'll use the word "intranet" or the phrase "effective intranet" to optimize a certain page. For the purposes of our discussion, we'll use search engine optimization, since it is used often in the field, and we'll use the abbreviation SEO. Search engine optimization has been unfairly treated as the ugly duckling within digital marketing. One of the reasons is that there have been quite a few corporations that have tried to fool search engines with various unallowable techniques. Most companies adhere to the guidelines set out by the search engines, but really it's just a matter of reading up on the rules that exist before calling in a search engine consultant.

Search engine optimization has also been thought of as something too technical and complicated for boards of directors, marketing departments and traditional advertising agencies. An ideal scenario would be that search engine optimization would form the basis for all marketing, not just digital. As mentioned earlier, it's one of the only marketing formats where the target groups look for ads. It's also related to other types of media, such as TV. If a news program talks about a tsunami, the number of searches for "tsunami" will increase after the program. We use search engines when we have questions that arise from ads, programs and articles from other media.

## Build a Search Engine-friendly Website

Searching is a continuous process. It never rests. To be a part of it, it's time to forget old-fashioned brochure-websites. What is needed now is a website with a suitable content and publishing strategy built on a solid technical foundation. The following five steps provide a good basis for a modern website:

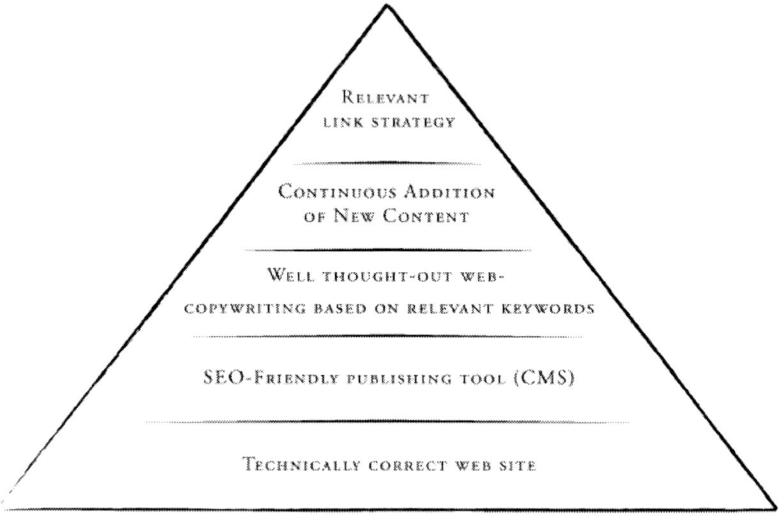


PICTURE 12. Five steps to ensuring a search engine-friendly website

The steps should be followed from the bottom up. First, "Technically correct website," then "Search engine-friendly publishing tool" and so on. The first two steps are introductory, while the last three are ongoing and never-ending. They should therefore be integrated into the daily work performed on the website.

## A Technically Correct Website

Most people think of a website as correct if it can be opened in a browser and if it's possible to navigate the website easily. However, it's not that simple. A search engine releases a little program called a search engine spider that navigates a website and looks for as many sites as possible to index. There is a difference between how a search engine spider works compared to a usual web browser. The search engine spider, or search engine robot, is not at all as forgiving as a web browser. The spider can't manage some of the techniques used on modern websites, which means it is possible for a web developer to mistakenly restrict access to the website by a spider. There are some basic rules that need to be followed in order to avoid this problem.

From a search engine perspective, there cannot be any frames on the website. In spite of this, there are a number of web shops that still use frames. It's easy to see if a website has frames if the menus and the text have their own scroll bars.

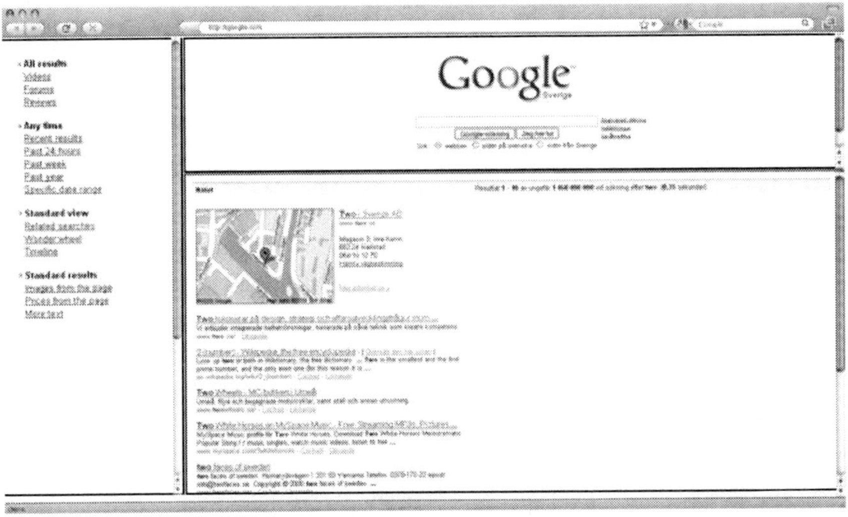


PICTURE 13. Example of a page with frames

Pages that are built with frames can be made to work in search engines, but it requires a lot of work by the developer, and makes it difficult for the visitor.

The pages on the website must be built according to a standard[12]. It's always a good starting point to build using some of the stricter standards that are out there. When a standard is chosen, it can be validated (checked for eventual faults) via different web tools[13]. A standard is

12 Current standards can be found at www.w3.org/html/.

13 One example is validator.w3.org

also useful from an accessibility perspective. There are many different types of web browsers. Web browsers for the blind work much better when a website is built according to a standard and validated against it. If the website is built from a web standard, then you'll likely find the right composition of headings in the text of the web page.

Avoid techniques that don't allow a search engine to look in menus and navigation bars. Techniques such as Adobe Flash and JavaScript, among others, can block certain pages from the search spider. It's best to simply build a website without a bunch of technical things in the navigation. The navigation should be clean links, without unnecessary functions. The risk with having complicated navigation is that it will hinder not only the search engine, but also the visitor. Of course, search engines are continuously upgrading their techniques and are getting better and better at handling the problems we've outlined above. In spite of that, it's not a good idea to use techniques that can hinder make things difficult for the user in the navigation bar.

Make sure that the pages on the website reply with the right http code[14]. Http means "hypertext transfer protocol" and is simply a connection between the web browser and the web server, where the website is located. When a user looks for a website by writing in an address, a request for that website is sent to the server. If everything works, and the website (i.e. web page) exists, then the server replies with the code 200, and sends the html text to the web browser.

As visitors, we don't see that the website returns the code 200, we just see the page appear on the screen in the web browser. In those instances where the page doesn't exist, the server replies with the code 404, the page cannot be displayed. Different web browsers interpret this in different ways, but those familiar with Internet Explorer are most likely familiar with the text "Page cannot be displayed".

14 For a list of status codes, see www.w3.org/protocols/http/htresp.html

When a page that is indexed in a search engine is removed, it can take a while before the search engine removes it from its index. If the page ranks high in the search results, the visitor won't be able to find the page. Instead, an error message will show up saying that the page can't be displayed. When a page is removed, the webmaster simply redirects traffic to a new page. There are a few ways to do this. The two most common ways are 301 (the page has been moved permanently) and 302 (the page has been moved temporarily). 301 is acceptable from a search engine perspective, while 302 isn't. In spite of this, many content management tools mistakenly say that the page has been temporarily moved. How is a search engine spider supposed to interpret that? The page is temporarily gone, but will show up again soon? In some cases, this can be the plan, but should not be used for web pages that are used for positioning in search engines. Those pages must stay put, and not be removed now and then. When a page is deleted, the spider should be redirected to another chosen page through a 301. The search engine then takes the power that the search engine has placed on that page and transfers it to the new page. All the visitors that have that page in their favourites will also be redirected, and avoid seeing a disappointing 404: the page cannot be displayed. A web editor should be able to create that function in the course of everyday maintenance of the website.

Every website has to have a so-called robots.txt[15]. This is a text file that lies at the root of the website and tells the search engine spider what areas the spider is not allowed to visit. If there are no such areas, the file still needs to exist, to say that all areas are accessible.

There are many traps for search engine spiders when the technical platform is created for a website. There are new and exciting techniques available all the time, and you have to be sure to build a website that will let spiders in and make the website available.

15 More information about robots.txt can be found at www.robotstxt.org.

## Search Engine-Friendly Content Management Tools

With regards to search engines, the choice of content management tools is critical. There are some tools that aren't appropriate because they lack search engine support. For example, it should be possible to insert a so-called "title tag." A title tag is the uppermost field in the web browser. It's also the field that is shown when a visitor adds a page as a favourite, and the field shown in a search engine's result list. Don't confuse the title tag with the headline of the website – they're two separate things.

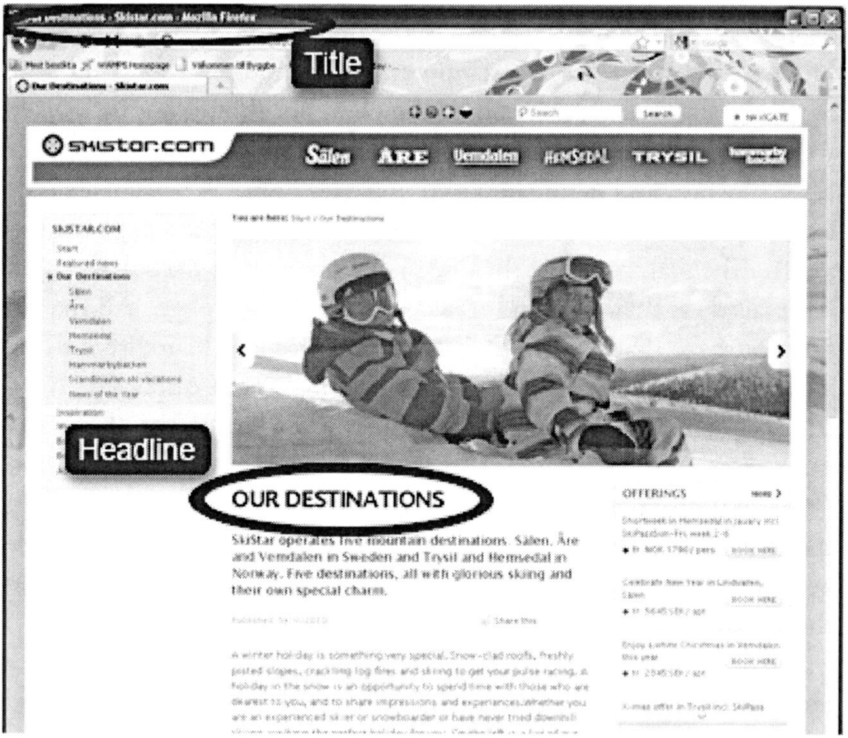


PICTURE 14. Examples of a title tag and a headline on a website.

The web editor should also be able to add an html tag called Meta Description, which is a description of the web page, and Meta Keywords, which are the four or five most important words on the page. Meta Description isn't visible to the visitor – it's hidden among the html codes. It's most often the field that is shown under the headline in the results of a search engine search. Meta Keywords are hardly ever used by search engines because they traditionally have been used to insert words that aren't actually on the web page in an attempt to trick search engines. Search engines often change their algorithms (formulas for how to rank a web page in the results list), and it's therefore a good idea to fill in a few words for the page in Meta Keywords. Be aware, however, that those words must appear on the web page.

The editor should also keep an eye on the address of the web page. When a page is ready to be published, the editor should be able to put the file name and search path to the page. There are limits created by the content management tool, but if an editor wants to create a page about peaches, the path to the page should look roughly like this:

www.webstrategyfundamentals.com/fruit/peaches.html
or
www.webstrategyfundamentals.com/fruit/peaches

There are of course variations depending on the publishing tool being used, but the word peaches should be able to be inserted for a page that talks about peaches.

Finally, the editor should be able to insert redirections when pages are moved or deleted. She does this via the 301 redirection, as described above under "A Technically Correct Website".

## Well-Planned Web Copy Based on Relevant Keywords

The web editor's job is to write firstly for the visitor, secondly for the search engine. In other words, she needs to write a text that works for both target groups. It's usually easier to write for the visitor, but the challenge is to have the search engine in mind too. Fortunately enough, editors no longer have to repeat the same word over and over again to ensure that the page will rank high in the results list. Nowadays, it requires a little more finesse and knowledge to rank highly. There isn't usually a great difference between a search engine-optimized text and one that's not, as long as the text and, most importantly, the keywords or phrases are in the right place.

There are a lot of different types of pages on a website. Not all of them are meant to rank highly in search engine results. When there are certain pages that need to rank highly, the web editor needs to think carefully. It's important to use the same words that the visitor has previously identified during the keyword analysis. When the right words are chosen, there are a few rules as to how the page should be created. It's about basic ground rules, and it's up to the editor to keep up with the changes that happen in the search engine's algorithms. The points described below are the most basic, and the minimum that is required to perform search engine work on a web site. We've talked earlier about the different fields that need to be filled in when a web editor creates a page. There are a few simple rules to be followed in that process:

1. A *titel tag* and *main headline (H1)* on the page cannot be identical.
2. *The Meta Description* cannot be copied from the text. It needs to be a short description of the page.
3. *The Meta Keywords* cannot contain any word that is **not** on the page.
4. Use the *keyword* early on in the text.
5. The *keyword* should be the word that appears most often in the text, not including so-called stop words, such as the, to, and, in.

Remember as well that the title tag is the text that a visitor will click on in the search engine's results. It should sell, and attract the visitor to click and visit the website.

Pay attention to the fact that algorithms, the search engines rules, are constantly changing. The rules described above are ground rules, and a web editor needs to keep up-to-date with the changes that occur, and the impact it has on her work. To obtain relevant knowledge, it's important to visit forums, blogs and search engine guidelines pages. To get you started, see the list of links at www.webstrategyfundamentals.com.

## Continuous Addition of New Content

Search engines and visitors love new content. The clear trend with search engines is that they prefer a website that is updated often over a more static website. The functions in the search engine are evolving in response to the fact that visitors can choose how "fresh" they want to the content to be in the results list. In many cases, the visitor is looking for current content, not the old websites that often top the list of results. A web editor needs to have a strategy as to how often something will be published on the website, and have an idea about where on the website the new content will be published. It's important to note that not all new content has to be written and optimized for search engines. It could be another type of content, such as news and other texts that only exist for a short period of time. It's more important that visitors and search engines see that there is something new happening on the web site, and that the content is growing and changing. **Create a strategy for how often something will be published, and, if possible, spread it out over time.** Remember that new content is just that – new – and it means creating new pages. In other words, you can't handle new content by changing a few pages now and then for a little change; new pages need to be added.

## Application of Link Strategy

Before the launch of Google in 1998, search engines indexed their web pages based solely on the content, i.e. the text on the page. Google created a small revolution by counting the links to the website in addition to content. The theory was that the more people who linked to a particular web page, the more people preferred that web page over the competition's, which led to a better position in the results list. Not only are links to the organization's website/web pages important, but also internal links on the website. Google even looks at links from the website.

To understand the importance of links to a website, there are many numbers of examples. Let's look at a slightly odd, perhaps even humorous, example, from former president George W. Bush. For a while, he ranked as number one on google.com for the word "failure", a word that didn't appear in the biography about Bush, which was the number-one ranking page on whitehouse.gov for the phrase. The reason Bush was at the top was that many bloggers in the US had decided to link to the page on whitehouse.gov with the text "miserable failure" in the link text. Soon enough, George W. Bush was the top hit with the words "miserable failure" and it didn't take long before it was enough to type "failure". In other words, it was possible to manipulate Google into giving a web page top place with a word that didn't even exist on the page in question. Google of course reacted. After a while, they sent out information that, to rank high, it wasn't enough to link to a page with specific text in the link – the text also had to appear on the page. Proof for this was that George W. Bush would no long rank first under "failure". In the mean time, it seemed that Google blocked only that particular example. The search engine consultant branch quickly found other words that worked in exactly the same way. Try it yourself. Search for "click here" and see if Adobe Acrobat is the first result to be listed. If it's not, then Google re-examined their routines, and actually found a long-term solution; otherwise they've blocked yet another gratifying example in the world of search engines.

### External Links

Now that we've looked at the power of links, let's take a closer look at how a web editor should think about working with links. Links are hard to control, but with a bit of groundwork and planning, the work can handle and develop itself. Of course, the following example very much depends on the type of organization that owns the website, as well as the size of the staff and budget available. It's important that the link work is consistent through all areas of the organization. In this way, the built-up link work can more or less manage itself. Natural areas for laying link groundwork are press releases, sponsoring, and business partners. Never send out a press release without first optimizing it for search engines; include deep links (links to a page further down in the structure of a website) to important pages with relevant keywords in the text. Use one of the many websites available for publishing press releases. Without too much effort, the organization now has a number of excellent links.

Other sources for external links include sponsoring. Each occurrence of sponsoring should have one or more links from the sponsored partner. You can create a few appropriate texts that include links that will tell the people you are sponsoring that they should easily be able to publish their own texts with the right links to the right sources. The same is true for business partners and other sources where you are in control of the linkage. The best situation is when the source of the link is about the same thing as your own website. If your website is about horses, it's great to have links from other horse-related websites. Links from larger websites are often better than from smaller and lesser known. Always strive for that golden link – the one from the leading website from the field you're working in. If the website's goal is to sell a certain product, a link from the product's manufacturer is a golden link, especially if none of the other competitors have managed to obtain it.

If you have a website that interests bloggers, it's a good idea to help them with their work. Make sure you have pictures in various formats (width and height) so that they are compatible with the most common blogging tools, and give bloggers permission to use them. Make sure that they link back to you, as a thank you. Be sure that your trademark appears in the pictures, and be clear about how often they can use the pictures – even if they are free.

The external link work is a continuous process, and should have someone in charge of it. The words that will be deep-linked are the words that don't rank highly in search engines' result lists.

## Internal Linking Within the Website

Besides linking from external pages, you can have internal linking. This means linking from one page to another within your own website. It's not the links in the navigation, headers or footers that are important, it's the ones that appear in the block text. Let's assume that there is a page on a website that talks about roses.

PICTURE 15. Example of internal linking

It's the page from the website that ranks highest in a search engine search done on the word roses, which makes it a perfect target for a link from another page. When the web editor writes another page, and uses the word roses in the text, then that word, roses, should be made into a link to the page about roses

Of course, it's not a good idea to have too many internal links. Likewise, internal linking isn't made only for search engines, it's also a service to the visitor, and should therefore be relevant. It's up to the visitor to choose if she wants to keep reading, or click the link to jump to another page on the website. The web editor is the one who decides how many internal links to have on the page, but three or four tends to be the maximum for a text that covers one and a half A4 pages. Too many links makes the text difficult to read. An adequate amount gives the visitor the possibility to choose, when she comes to a link in the text. It could even be an advantage if the visitor has come to the wrong page, and wants to read about roses, not rose hips. In this instance, an early link on the page about rose hips will point the visitor in the right direction for roses.

### Links from the Website to Other Websites

Lastly, you can link from your website to other sites. It's always good to give your visitor the option to read more about a certain topic. By linking to other websites, the visitor can further investigate something that the organization can't provide, either through lack of opportunity or time. For example, a car dealership can often not compete with the functions offered by the manufacturer or the distributor. For the visitor, a visit to another website gives added value which improves the image of the organization's own brand. Of course there is a risk that you'll lead the visitor away from your website, but it's worth it, since such a link helps the visitor to make a decision. Again, the links are there mostly for the benefit of the visitor, not the search engine. Pleasing the search engine should be seen as a bonus effect.

## Summary of Search Engine Optimization

Search engines are becoming more and more important. It's not uncommon that 50 to 60 percent of the traffic that arrives on the website doesn't come to the website's homepage. Each individual page is a potential start page. The importance of search engines increases because we as individuals look more and more for information. An organization has to decide whether they will hire an expert for the work needed for search engines. As always, it's about how many people the organization has at its disposal, and how they can be put to best use. In the book "The Truth About Search Engine Optimization" by Rebecca Lieb , there is a great comparison for pros and cons with using your own staff versus bringing in an outsider. Among the pros is that search word positioning is closely tied to the content on a website, and therefore beneficial if the one responsible for the search engine can work closely with the web editor. This gives much higher productivity. Among the cons is that it's hard for an internal person with various job assignments to keep up with the developments that constantly occur with regards to how a search engine works. One of the advantages of bringing in outside help is that the search engine optimization company has staff that are focused on the task, and makes you less dependent on your own personnel. The downside of this is, of course, the cost, and in some cases it's not always clear what the consultant does. Transparency between the search engine consultant and the client is a must. If the consultant won't provide that, then she shouldn't be doing the job. Oftentimes it's not about whether the search engine work should be done internally or externally. A good team includes web editors that work with a search engine team, where they together draw out the guidelines for how the search engine work should be done.

## Attracting Visitors via Banner Ads

Banners are the oldest form of Internet advertising. It's a way to capture visitors while also promoting a brand. Each time a banner is shown to a visitor, your brand gets exposure. Unfortunately, it's becoming more and more common that banners resemble a TV commercial in their construction. This type of banner doesn't work if the goal is to increase traffic. They're often messy, and risk that the visitor will just ignore a banner that delivers the wrong message at the wrong time. To be clicked, a banner needs to be simple, and give the visitor a clear idea of why she should click, and what she'll get when she does. **A banner lies in the visitor's peripheral vision, and needs to capture her attention when she's actually looking for something else within the content of the website she's visited.** Det är viktigt att bannern är i rätt läge när besökaren är på väg förbi. It's important that the banner is in the right phase when the visitor is on her way down the page. If the banner tells a story through a film or "slideshow", without showing a brand name, the risk is that the visitor will move on without having seen the sender, in which case the effect of building the brand name is lost. It's also possible that the amount of clicks on such a banner will be quite low. An example of a banner that tells a story is the following:

PICTURE 16. A story-telling banner. Who is the sender?

You can't see who is sending the banner, and you can't see what it's selling or advertising. It's not computers – it just happens to be a computer in the banner. However, as visitors, we're supposed to stay calm for some reason. The hope is that we as visitors will be caught up in the banner's "mystique" and click. Here's another example of a banner that gets right to the point:

PICTURE 17. Example of a converted all-in-one banner.

The sender is easy to identify, as is what the visitor gets when she clicks on the banner. This is a converted banner, a banner that is designed to increase traffic. It's aimed at delivering a clear message, and it clearly communicates what a visitor will get out of a visit, i.e. what the goal is with the campaign. It also displays your brand name, since a visitor can easily see the coke bottles, and the name Coke. These types of banners are gaining ground. It's more and more about capturing visitors than making a banner that will win all kinds of advertising awards. Clarity needs to increase, since experienced Internet users claim not to "see banners." With the help of banner campaign statistics, this can easily be disproved. Most people who use the web have clicked on a banner, and they will keep clicking as long as the message feels right at the time they see the banner.

A banner can be bought in four different ways. They are:

- to buy a place for a specified amount of time
- to pay for a certain number of views
- to pay for a certain number of clicks
- to pay for a result

The first point is about buying a spot for the banner during a limited time period. The second option is that the advertiser pays for the banner to be shown a certain number of times. A showing is the same thing as displaying, which is another word that is used in this context. In the third option, the advertiser pays for an actual click by a visitor. Finally, the advertiser only pays for the visits that have generated a result, i.e. a purchase, booking or order. The last two options are the most attractive for the advertiser from an expense perspective. The advertiser knows how many visitors or results are needed to generate income. Despite the advantages, paying by click or result is quite uncommon – most ad space is sold by time or number of displays. There are ad networks that buy up attractive ad space by impression, and then sell them per click, which is a lucrative way to buy good ad space, and gives the added advantage of only paying per click by the visitors. There are also networks that sell per views and here your banner is widespread at first and after a while the placement focuses on the different sites where the banners get the most clicks.

## Sponsored links in Search Engines

These days, most search engines have a sponsored area, where you can buy space. A sponsored link shows up in different locations depending on the search engine, but what they all have in common is that they are in some way marked as sponsored or paid links.

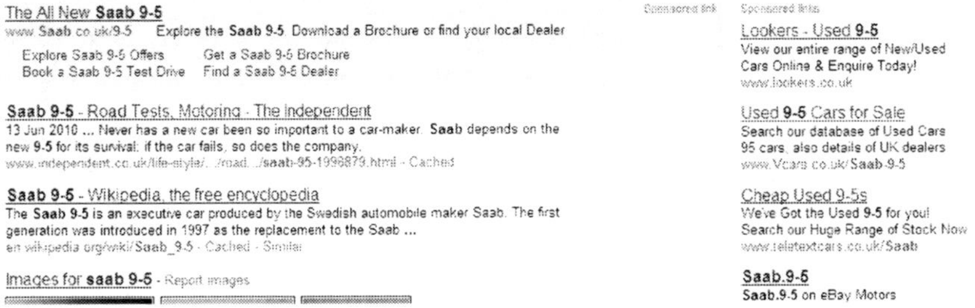


PICTURE 18. Sponsored links at the top of the results list (one link) and 4 to the right.

An advertiser creates an advertisement with an advertising text. Words are connected to the ad, and when those words are searched for in the search engine, the ad will hopefully show up. What I mean by hopefully is that some words have stiff competition, and the ad will likely share the space with more advertisements than actually fit in the space, which means that your ad may not show up every time the word is searched in the search engine. Payment is made when a visitor clicks on the ad, and is sent to the advertiser's website. This payment model is called Pay per Click (PPC). In other words, it's free as long as no one clicks on a link. Competition for sponsored links is steadily increasing. More and more advertisers want to attach an ad to a word. Space is limited, making it more difficult to control traffic with that word. Having a word end up in an advantageous position leading to positive outcomes in terms of click cost requires a lot of knowledge on the part of the person leading the campaign. Other branches and words can be without sponsored content, and it doesn't require as much knowledge in order to succeed.

An advertiser can also place her ads on different content networks. For example, Google has a network of different websites that rent out parts of their space to show ads. The websites share their income per click with Google, and earn money by having sponsored links on their websites. The advertiser can choose which websites her ads will be shown on.

A sponsored link is profitable when a visitor is close to making a decision, and is therefore searching for something specific in a search engine. It's one of the few times when someone is actively looking for advertisements. The chances of making that visitor into a customer are greater than when the visit comes from a banner ad or another type of passive advertising. Sponsored links should therefore be considered active marketing.

## Electronic Newsletters

According to Wikipedia[16] , a newsletter is "a regularly distributed publication generally about one main topic that is of interest to its subscribers." An electronic newsletter is distributed via the Internet to a subscriber's e-mail address.

**Newsletters are first and foremost a way to take care of existing customers and to pique their interest.** For a relatively low cost, it's possible to take care of an established group of customers. In other words, it's a cheap way to have the customers generate more business. Of course, it is also possible to work with new customers through newsletters. However, the Personal Data Act[17]of Sweden for instance, places certain restrictions about who can be sent information and other countries have similar laws. Before a campaign starts, you should go over the rules about how e-mail addresses are collected.

Newsletters have a good relationship between expense and income. They are also relatively easy to send, and most newsletter components have good statistical features so that you can see how many have received the newsletter, how many have opened it, and how many have acted in some way because of what they read.

## Links from Other Websites

Links are one of the cornerstones of the web. They give the visitor the possibility to easily jump between different pages on a website or to move from one website to another. Links are important for many reasons. They provide a way for a search engine to judge the popularity of a certain page, but they also generate visitors. If the link lies within the same subject area, then it's also possible that the visitor is of

16 Wikipedia is an online encyclopaedia that is updated by Internet users, and can be found at en.wikipedia.org

17 For more information about the Personal Data Act, see www.datainspektionen.se (information available only in Swedish)

a higher quality. There are websites where you can publish press releases, in which it's beneficial to place links to other parts of the website. Another way to have links to websites within the same subject area is to look at the blogging world, and try to get good links from there.

## The Social Web

The social web is a way to give people with common interests the possibility to share information and to discuss different subjects with each other. The social web is nothing new, because the web has always been social. Even before the web was in use, we used the Internet to exchange experiences and to help each other with problems and questions. The basis for today's online forums comes from something called Usenet from 1979. Usenet was a way to communicate over the Internet through an e-mail-like client (Usenet-client), and participate in various debates and forums. It was possible to post questions and answers just like in today's web-based threaded forums. In other words, the Internet has always been social, but the opportunities for the social web have increased exponentially and the platforms have become simpler. There are social networks, forums and websites where you can rate things, make price comparisons and much more. There are marketing opportunities on the paid market, but there are also free ways to generate more visitors from the social web. The paid options include ads in the form of sponsored links, a combination of sponsored links and banners, and of course actual banner ads. New variations and possibilities for advertising pop up all the time.

One aspect of the social web are social bookmarks. Social bookmarks were created when web users got tired of bookmarks in a web browser being attached to a specific computer and browser. When someone sat by her work computer, and created a bookmark or a favourite, it was connected to the work computer. If she booted up her home computer, the bookmark was not available. So, functions were created on the web where you could place your bookmarks and have access to them from any computer, as long as the computer could connect to the Internet. The service was expanded so that a user could get tips and suggestions for other good websites based on the links she had posted herself. To make it easier for social bookmarking, it's a good idea to create a list of links with social bookmarks on each page of the website, and give the visitor the option to link via her social networks or her bookmark website (Delicious, StumbleUpon and Digg are examples of social bookmark sites).

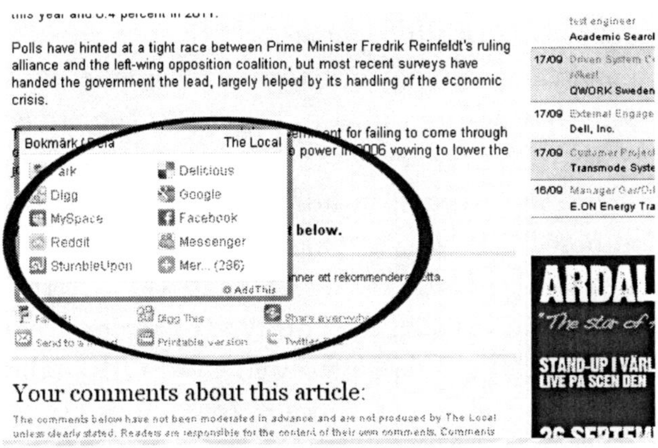


PICTURE 19. Länkar till sociala nätverk från vf.se.

New websites and internet-based functionalities pop up all the time. Having a strategy to deal with the social web is a must. First and foremost, surveillance is important. Where is the organization and its brand(s) discussed? The next step comes when that has been established. It's about outlining a strategy for how the organization will handle these discussions. An involvement in the social web that is too swift will often fall flat. The strategy for what happens on the web, outside of the organization's own website deserves to have a whole book devoted to the subject, and there will eventually be someone who will write it.

## Long-Term Versus Campaign-based Internet Marketing

In Internet marketing, we differentiate between two different branches: long -term and campaign-based marketing. Long-term marketing is based on actively working with the website, its content and links to increase traffic and attract new visitors. Campaign-based marketing is more short-term and takes place during short time periods with a clear goal and purpose. Briefly, a campaign is about directing a certain target group to a website where the target group will perform some form of action to become a customer. This type of campaign can be quite simple in its shape. It could be a few well-chosen ads in the sponsored section of a search engine that land the visitor on specially chosen pages on the website. It could also be large integrated campaigns with lots of different sources that together create a whole.

In short, search engine optimization and newsletters are two ways to conduct long-term Internet marketing. Banners, sponsored links, social media announcements and other paid announcements are examples of campaign-based marketing. One of the biggest differences is that, with search engine optimization, the visitor has to come to one page on the website. In the other instances, it's up to the marketer to choose the landing site for the visitor.

## Choosing a Landing Site

There are four different ways to land a campaign. They are:

- to land on the homepage of the website
- to land on one unique page of the website
- to land on a special landing page
- to land on a special campaign website, apart from the website

### Landing on the Homepage of a Website

The least attractive option of the above named choices is the website's homepage. It is still, however, one of the most common choice in badly managed campaigns with sponsored links. A visitor clicks on a link in a search engine, and expects to land on a page that gives her the information she was looking for. The back button on the mouse or in the web browser can then be very close to being the next click. She doesn't want to start looking again. Imagine that a visitor has searched for engineer, and lands on this website:

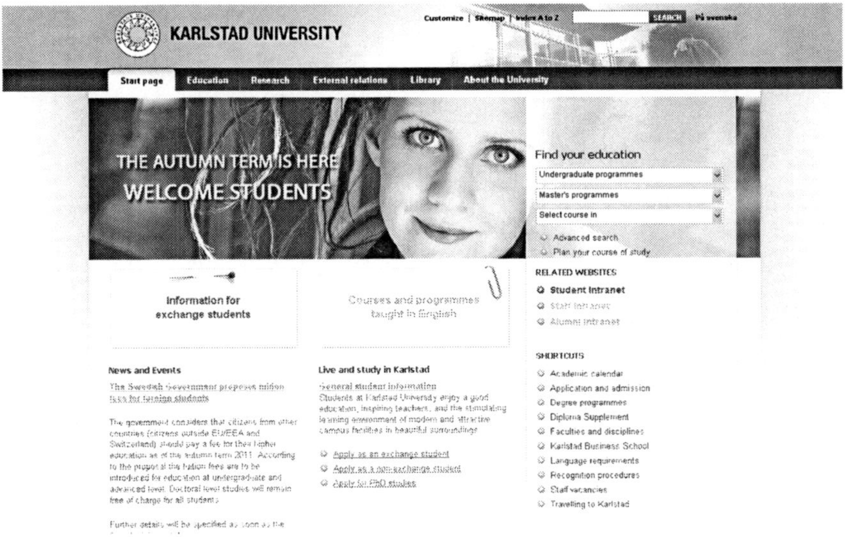


PICTURE 20. The homepage as a landing page for a campaign.

Now the visitor needs to start looking for the engineering program again. If she can't quickly find the "Education" portal, there is a risk that she will go back to the search engine results and that the next link in the results list will be visited

## Landing on One Unique Page of the Website

A more attractive approach is to land the visitor on a page that deals with engineering education:

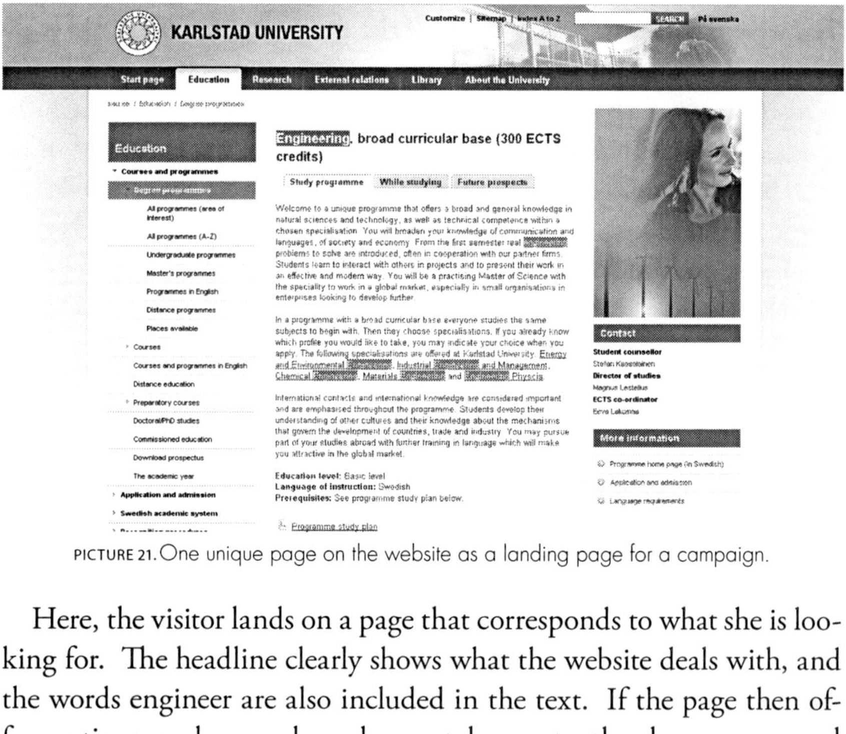


PICTURE 21. One unique page on the website as a landing page for a campaign.

Here, the visitor lands on a page that corresponds to what she is looking for. The headline clearly shows what the website deals with, and the words engineer are also included in the text. If the page then offers options, such as apply, order a catalogue etc, the chances are good that the visitor will become a customer. It's also important to give the visitor the option of navigating further to other pages that could be of interest to her.

## Landing on a Special Landing Page

If the campaign has a clear goal, then a special landing page could be an alternative. A goal could include being able to apply directly, order a catalogue or something else where the visitor needs to accomplish something or make a decision. Here's an example of a landing page:

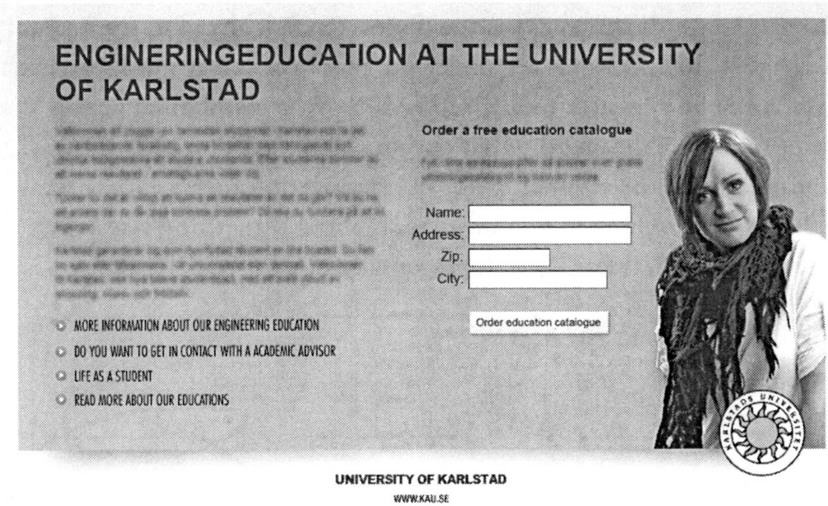


PICTURE 22. A special landing page that can only be reached through the campaign.

Here, there is a clear goal with the page: the visitor is meant to fill in the form and order a catalogue. Naturally the form will use only those fields necessary to be able to send a catalogue: name, address, postcode and district.

It would be good to get an e-mail address and perhaps also a telephone number. However, it may be best not to ask for such information, since the chances are greater that more visitors will hesitate. They don't want to risk receiving unwanted e-mails, SMS or phone calls. It's better to follow up with this information in the next step, when there is a clear response that the request has been received, and a catalogue will arrive within a certain number of working days. On that page, it can be possible to request an e-mail address or a telephone number for more information via e-mail, SMS, MMS, or perhaps to be contacted by a study advisor. It has been shown that we are more likely to provide more personal information after we have initially given out a little. Be careful, then, with what is asked for when such forms are used on different pages on a website. Another thing to note on the landing page shown above is the option to click ahead to the ordinary website. The links that are under the text take the visitor to the website, and the statistics tool is set to count the number of people that choose to take that road. That option should exist for the visitor who, for one reason or another is not quite ready to order a catalogue, but who wants to know more information about something else before an order is placed. Here is another example of a form:

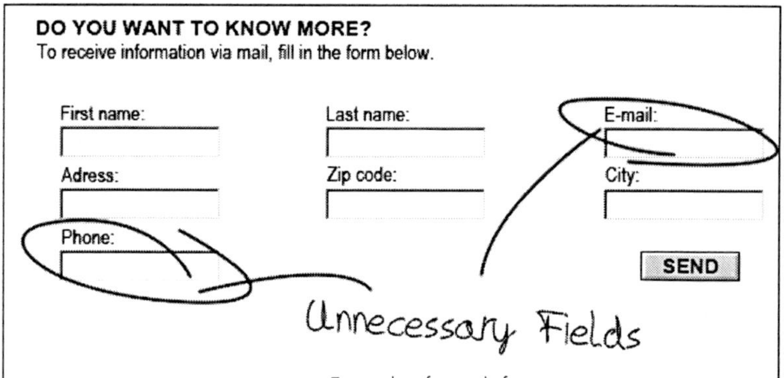


PICTURE 23 Example of a web form

Read the instructions carefully: "To receive information via mail, fill in the form below." There are two fields that are not needed. When something will be sent using standard mail services, the fields for telephone number and e-mail are unnecessary. They are there because the customer information system requires them, or because "they can be good have." The chances are that those fields will scare away the visitors that don't want to share such information. Additionally, it's better to have the first name and surname together in one field. Again, it's likely that it's the customer relationship management system that is setting these restrictions because the first name and surname need to be separated in the database. A common source of error is that the entire name ends up in the first name field, and the surname field is empty. Naturally, there should be a screening process to ensure that no field is left empty, but this can be a source of irritation for the visitor, and increases the risk that the visitor will leave the website, rather than correct the information. There are various different types of visitors. There are those that will endure all sorts of oddities, because they want nothing more than to perform the task needed to become a customer. There are also those that realise immediately that this was not for them and disappear. Then there are also the uncertain ones, the ones that don't have time, and the ones who aren't completely secured, i.e. the ones that, met with certain obstacles, leave with no clear intent to come back. It's for the last group that a form should be created. The announcer wants to have as high of a yield as possible for her campaign. She wants as many visitors as possible to complete the goal for the campaign.

## Landing on a Campaign Website

For some larger campaigns, a so-called campaign website is used for landing. Such a website is often created using Flash techniques, and is likely quite advanced in terms of functions and options. The time for really large campaign websites is nearing its end. In those instances where a campaign website is created nowadays, it's often on a much smaller scale, with very specific functions. It's also often a result of the limitations of the normal website that can't provide the options that a campaign website can. An example of when it is okay to use a campaign website is for contests. In those cases, the campaign website is ideal, since it offers the space needed to handle a contest in all its shapes. Another occasion where a campaign website can be used is when there is a need to differentiate between the usual website and what the campaign is about, such as a limited time offer.

## Relating Offline Advertising to the Web

All marketing that an organization does in media outside the web and the Internet will sooner or later impact what is done on the website. The worst-case scenario is that a radio ad can lead visitors to the competition; a TV-campaign designed to improve a brand name could damage it, if those that see the campaign search for it in a search engine, but don't end up on the intended website.

Traditionally, there are two extremes within advertising: strategic advertising (i.e. brand improving), and tactical advertising (business generating advertising, also called convergence marketing). An advertisement can be placed between these two extremes on a scale:

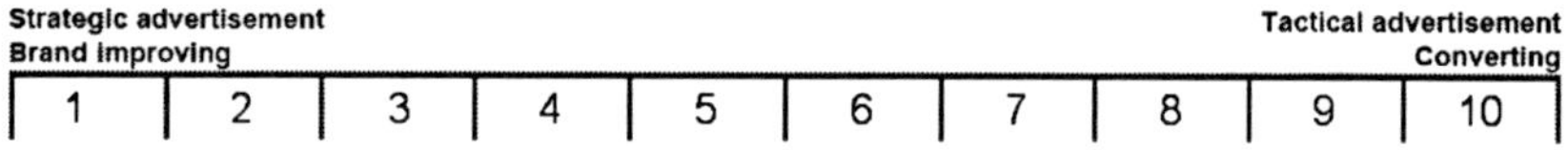


PICTURE 24. Rosen Velocity Scare by Richard G. Rosen

In those cases where an advertisement is intended to improve a brand, there are a lot of TV-ads where the brand isn't shown until the end of the film, when it is shown in full force to the viewer. In tactical advertising, it's about selling a service or a product at a good price, and to have as many viewers as possible buy in. According to old dogmas in the advertising industry, these extremes can't be combined. And yet we're seeing more and more examples of this happening, and it is something we're going to see more and more of, as the scale shown above is blurred and ads need to be both brand building and tactical. One of the more important causes behind this development is that visitors want to know how to buy the product. The research we mentioned earlier from Jupiter Research[18] shows that two thirds of viewers go online to search for information after having seen some form of advertisement through other media. In other words, it's about exposing the company's trademarks and/or products in the ad. Then, you have to know which words and products were used in the ad. What happens when someone searches for a word from the ad, or a product name that isn't the brand name? In other words, you have to be responsible for the campaign for the entire time. More often than not, all campaigns will sooner or later end up on the web. The sender needs to make sure that the receiver lands on the right place on the web, and, above all else, on the right website.

## Consider the Content of the Advertisement

If the advertisement has content that is easy to remember, it will surely be that which a receiver will use to search, if she can't remember the sender. It could be words in the slogan, words that were repeated, or words on the product that aren't the trademark. Test these words and word combinations in a search engine before you send out the advertisement. If you don't get a good result, it's time to gain some coverage with sponsored links that catch those words. If unique word combinations pop up, it could be worth it to secure those combinations by buying domain names – if they're available. If they are already in use, consider whether that website is good or bad for the organization.

A unique domain name has the advantage of making a campaign measurable. It could be a domain name that is only shown on certain channels, and, if it's measurable, can be followed up on online, even if it started offline. The same goals can be achieved by using the domain name with an addition.

Example: www.webstrategyfundamentals.com/campaignname.

18 Jupiter Research: iProspect Offline Channel Influence on Online Search Behavior Study (August 2007)

Such an assault approach also makes the campaign measurable. It's about taking the campaign to the goal: from the message in the advertisement to a successful customer who has completed the goal for the campaign.

## Summary of Having Visitors Come to a Website

A lot of what an organization sends out in terms of advertising, messages, and information will generate searches on the web. Working strategically with attracting the right visitors to a website is a larger job than most organizations realize. Web users are becoming more frequent users of search engines. Normal advertising strategies are devised with the goal to have a visitor know about the organization's name and the trademark's name (i.e. brand awareness), and to have the visit start on the website's homepage. On average, 50 to 60[19] percent of all visits to a website won't start on the homepage. This means that all pages on a website are potential homepages, and need to be treated as such.

A visit on a website often starts with a search in a search engine. Soon, it won't be an option not to work strategically with search engines. Working at positioning an organization's website highly in the results list from a search engine is a job that spans across more than one department of an organization. Searching has also become the simplest way to find information, which means that when a visitor has landed on a website, she will continue to search with the internal search engine. It's a good idea to monitor these searches to learn more about a visitor's needs, in terms of texts on the website.

Searching isn't the only way to attract visitors to a website. Internet marketing is much broader than that. New opportunities are constantly showing up, and many campaigns that are run through traditional media are also being pushed on the Internet. This is naturally the way it should be, but there needs to be a constant "noise" on the Internet that exposes the trademark in different places. This could be in the form of newsletters, sponsored links and tactically placed banners or other forms of web and Internet-based advertisements that

19 Statistics are taken from ca. 50 websites that are analyzed monthly by Two (two.se)

are shown to the right target group. Noise exists as a constant background, and is a good complement to more time-controlled campaign-based marketing. Think also about how to carry over a message from traditional channels. Not every message can work in a banner, since other rules apply on the web, as compared to TV, radio or print.

# *Section 3.* Taking Care of Visitors and Turning them into Customers

The next step in a long-term Internet marketing strategy is to take care of the visitors and turn them into customers.

PICTURE 25. Taking care of the visitor and turning her into a customer

Structure and design on a website are built like a pyramid, where the customer is expected to start at the top (the homepage) and navigate her way down the structure. Today, statistics show that it's more common for a visit to start on a page other than the homepage. In spite of this knowledge, there is often more time and energy spent on how the homepage will be structured and designed than on the other pages of the website. Those who enter the website from the homepage are likely people who already know about the website. Those that come from a search engine or in some other way land on a page further down in the structure may not know about the website or the organization. A myth that we've already talked about and tried to debunk states that a visitor needs to find a page in three clicks at most. A visitor that doesn't find anything of value on a website rarely takes the time to click even once. On the other hand, as long as there is something to gain by her visit, the visitor is willing to click as many times as needed. When the trail goes cold, the visitor is back on the search engine's results lists, or the source she came from before she landed on the website. It has never been easier to click your way back to earlier pages in the web browser with the click of a mouse button. It's important to create a decent and clear navigation that supports the visitor and leads her to the right content. Of course it's better if this happens in as few clicks as possible, but it's still better to put your energy into making good hot trails. Use your energy to lead the visitor right rather than bending over backwards to make the content accessible in three clicks.A nice complement to the navigation is a search function, especially for those visitors that land on the homepage and are then supposed to find content on their own. The search function is also a goldmine for the one responsible for the editorial work on the website. It can provide insight into which words are most sought after, and whether or not the visitor had a hit on the search. It's also possible to adjust the search function to capture spelling errors, for example. A golden rule is that the website's functions should never work worse than the leader of the field. When a website wants to show films or film sequences, it should work just as well as the leading website for film clips; a search function should be just as good as the leading search engine, etc. Of course, this can be a challenge, but a visitor who is met with a lack of quality would rather go somewhere else.

## Goals with the Website

In section 1, we talked about the purpose and goals of a website. We discussed that a website has one or more general goals or purposes:

- to sell something
- to generate connections with customers
- to improve a brand
- to support and help customers

Besides the general goals, there should be more concrete goals. It is the achievement of these goals that give effect on the website. They provide a measurable value, which in turn generates revenue or some form of "income." For organizations that don't operate for profit, the goals can be about simplifying tasks for the staff by redirecting questions via phone and e-mail to the website.A website should always have measurable goals that can have some value attached to them. An example is a website that sells a product that isn't exactly appropriate to sell directly from a web shop, such as a car, or an air conditioner. The goal for that website is to have the customer fill in a contact form, or in some way contact the organization's sales people to generate business. You can set up a formula for the required steps to see the effect of the website.Initially, the website has 100 unique visitors per day. Of these, an average of one person out of 100 will fill in the contact form. Of the 100 contacts that come in, every fourth person will buy a product, which means approximately seven to eight transactions per month. What would happen if the number of unique visitors increased by 100? You can always reflect on whether it's the number of visitors that needs to increase, or if there needs to be some adjustments so that more visitors will take the step to become customers. Sometimes, the answer can be the first option; sometimes it's the latter. Oftentimes, it's a mixture of both. In any case, it's clear that there is money to be saved and/or earned by actively working with the goals and the degree to which these goals are reached. Consider the goals of the following website:

PICTURE 26. Goals for an e-business website

For an online bookshop, the goal is of course to sell books. They want the customer to place a book in their shopping cart and then proceed to the check out and pay. They also want a customer to purchase more books. That's why, at the bottom, there are tips on books that other buyers of "your" book have purchased.Consider the goals that this website has:

PICTURE 27. Goals for a car dealership

There are many small goals. At the time this picture was taken from the website, you couldn't purchase a car from a web shop. However, you could contact a salesperson, book a test drive or book a time for service. It's about small goals that all lead to the car company getting the chance to sell something to a visitor. The goals need to be clear and easy to achieve. By easy, I mean that the visitor needs to do as few things as possible for the goal to be reached. It shouldn't require an essay to book service, or unnecessary information to book a time for a test drive. What is the minimum information needed from a visitor when she fills in a form? If it becomes complicated, the visitor will go to another website where it's easier to become a customer. Examples of possible goals:

- order/purchase something
- a subscription to a newsletter
- a request for more information
- a download of a pdf or other document
- contact with someone
- a certain number of pages visited
- the amount of time the visitor spends on the website
- x percent of traffic generated by search engines
- the number of unique visitors over a period of time

There is merit in knowing which customers visit our website. The quantitative goals are measured with web statistics, but knowing the qualitative value requires more knowledge about the individual behind the visitor. The technique can't manage this, besides the fact that such information is protected by the Personal Data Act. There are statistical solutions that show which companies have visited the website, but not who visited. The best way to know more about the individuals is to attract them with something, such as a registration of some kind. Downloading a pdf-file that a customer really wants can be hidden behind a free or paid registration. Other goals are to mark important pages on a website and then track how many visitors pass through those pages. If we suspect that a certain type of visitor isn't using the contact form, there is the option of providing a specific telephone number beside the contact form, and then seeing how many calls come in that way. Setting up and monitoring goals should be used to calculate how much an organization is earning from the website. The expression used is return on investment (ROI), i.e. how big is the business value created on the website. If a website saves or creates business for a one million dollars, then hundred thousand dollar price tag is reasonable. If the return is zero, it's an expensive website. The point is to find the goals that give a good return on the organization's investment in the website.

## Managing Forms

As we've already talked about, it's important to think carefully about the structure and composition of fields in a form. While it's true that we have both a first and a last name, it's easiest to simply fill in a name, that is to say the entire name, in one field. The fields should be in a logical order, and be labelled clearly. A visitor shouldn't need to start wondering what should be filled in and why. Be clear with which fields are required, and which ones are optional. If a field is optional, maybe you don't need it.Remember that forms can help to qualify a visitor. As an example, let's look at a website for making reservation inquiries for conferences. In a form, the visitor fills in various details, including how many people the reservation is for. This information is valuable in the next step. The answers can be grouped according to the number of people included in the reservation. For example, when the group includes up to twelve people, the website will show a text saying that the visitor will be contacted within a certain period of time. If the group is from 13 to 30 people, the response time will be shorter, and for conferences with over 30 participants there will also be an online chat where the visitor can get an immediate answer and more information. The need to qualify visitors exists for many organizations, especially for those that have lots of inquiries via the website. There is also the possibility to have the forms adapt to the number of inquiries that come in. If there is a period of lots of inquiries, the form will "complicate" itself, and aim to reach only the most relevant, qualified customers. In times of fewer inquiries, the form will be automatically simplified and allow more inquiries to come in. A qualified visitor can also have more options in the next steps, compared to a visitor who isn't as profitable for the organization.A form calls for consideration and reflection. How it is designed depends on many different factors, where each situation is more than likely unique. The form needs to be designed for the right target group, with the right content, and can potentially change over time when factors in the surrounding environment change. Don't allow the work with a form to become routine, where everything is packed in simply because the information "can be good to have." Everything that is included in a form needs to be there for a reason.

## Leading the Visitor Right

A website needs to help the visitor achieve the goals. Clear structure and clear navigation are musts to take the visitor to the goals. What complicates matters is that the entire page is not visible to the visitor. In web-speak, we talk about "above the fold" and "below the fold." The terms originally come from the newspaper industry. When a newspaper reader took the paper from the mailbox in the morning, it was folded at least once. The text that was "above the fold" – in the paper's upper half – was seen as more important; less important was the text that the reader had to unfold the paper to read. The same concept applies to a web page. What the visitor sees immediately is "above the fold" and the content that's lower down, where the visitor has to scroll, is "below the fold." Where that "fold" is depends on the size of the screen and how much space the web browser allocates to content in relation to toolbars, menus and other things that are "good to have" at the top of the web browser. A designer needs to be aware of the target group, and know what the statistics say about the size of the screens being used.One of the trends is that the width more or less doesn't matter any more. Most of today's screens are wide enough for most types of content. We like to read texts that are between 55 and 70 characters wide, and today, that's not a problem. It's the height that still causes issues and will do so for the foreseeable future. We are becoming more and more portable in our choices of computers – sales of small and laptop computers are increasing. That type of computer often has a wide screen, but a severe limit in height[22]. We've already mentioned that one of the clearest formulated goals for a website is when something is going to be sold online. Where to you put the but-

22 The focus for this book is computers, not mobile phones, which place entirely different demands on how screen surface should be used.

tons for adding something to the shopping cart? Ideally they should be clearly visible regardless of whether the visitor scrolls up or down the page.

## Layout Standardization

When we get in a car, we know from experience that the steering wheel, the accelerator, the brake and the gearshift are in the same spot regardless of the car's make and model. It hasn't always been so, but car manufacturers have begun to use standard placing. We would be extremely uncertain if the brakes were on the right, and the accelerator was on the left. There would undoubtedly be serious consequences if a driver who was used to the opposite configuration were to go into traffic. Standards have started to be created on the web as well, with regards to object placement on the screen. The consequences of breaking those standards are not as serious as in the car example above, but the visitors will have a hard time finding what they are looking for on such a website, and that's bad enough. We've already pointed out that web design is not the focus of this book. The following sketches should therefore be seen simply as an illustration of a structure to lead the customer right.The structure in the following example is created for a single page on a website:

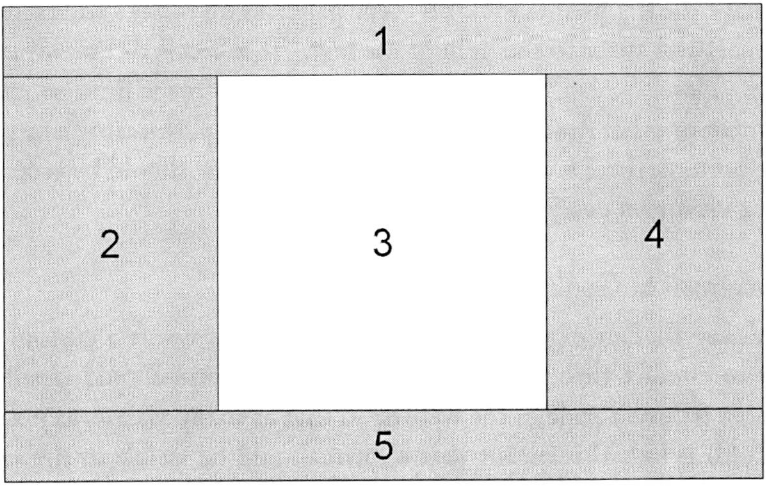


1. Header, containing among other things logotype and navigation
2. Left aligned menu
3. Content
4. Goals and possibilities to lead the visitor
5. Footer

In the header, we show a clear sender of the organization behind the website. Here we can find the overall navigation, or top navigation as its also known. If the website has a search function, this is a good place for it.A left menu has also become standard on modern and user-friendly websites. Exceptions are websites' start pages, such as home pages and the possible start pages for the various options in the top navigation. On these pages, the space is used to capture different target groups with "advertisements" and portals to content, which makes the left menu superfluous. There are, however, a number of websites, for example municipal, where top navigation is insufficient for showing the entire selection. It's in these instances where it's okay to have the left menu visible on every page. With today's wide screens, there is also space to the right of the text. This is called the conversion area. Here, we can find contact forms, links or image links to related content or other functions that build on a visitor performing a task. At the bottom, there is a footer with information that should be accessible for a visitor on every page of the website.

## Placement of Goals on the Page

Let's say that an organization has a website that wants a customer to get in contact through a form. The contact form should ideally be visible on every page of the website so that as many visitors as possible will fill it in. This means that a form should be visible in the upper part of the page when the visitor lands on the page:

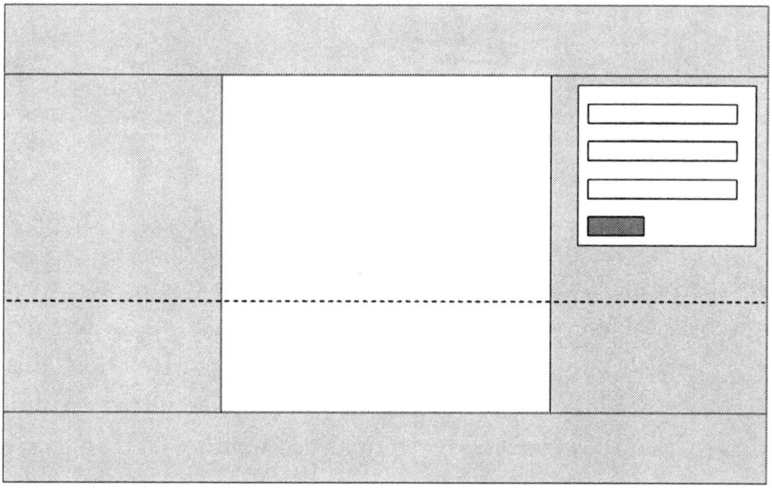

PICTURE 28. The dotted line shows what is "above the fold" and what is "under the fold"

In the image above, the contact form is clearly placed to the right of the text. It's easy to fill in the information required and send off the form. A contact form means that more visitors will contact the organization than if they need to follow an e-mail link or choose "Contact" in the menu, and then on to the form. It's mostly the hesitant visitors that the organization is likely to lose if the path to contact is too complicated. A link that opens an e-mail is considered more complicated than a simple form. If all the different contact options have been covered then the organization has done what it can to capture a visitor and turn her into a customer. If the form is at the top of the page, it could help to have a button at the bottom of the page that says "Contact us for more information". The reason is that many visitors want to read through the information on the page before a decision is made about contact, and in that case, it's nice to avoid scrolling to the top of the page to fill in the form.

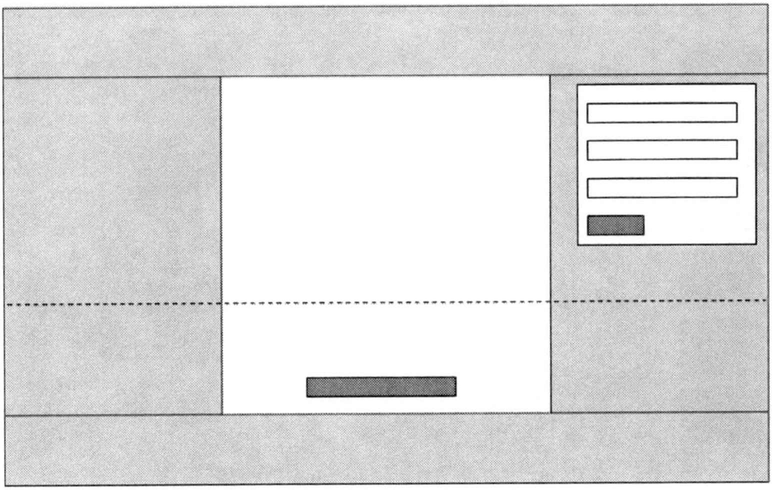

PICTURE 29. Picture with goals to the right and under the text.

Many website owners overlook what happens when a visitor reaches the end of the text. Here, there is an opportunity to guide the visitor further by showing different links to related content. We are lazy when it comes to looking for information on the web, and would rather not think or search too much to find good content. An important task for a web master is to test each page at different stages and consider the visitor's options for action. Of course, a web editor or a web master has specialist knowledge when it comes to content placement and structure. At the same time, our insight into the organization can make us blind to its faults. A visitor will always question what she gets out of a visit. She is looking for the kind of content that will change her from an interested visitor to a pleased visitor. Sometimes, an outside person can be better at looking at the website through a visitor's eyes, thereby noticing obvious faults. An example is this website:

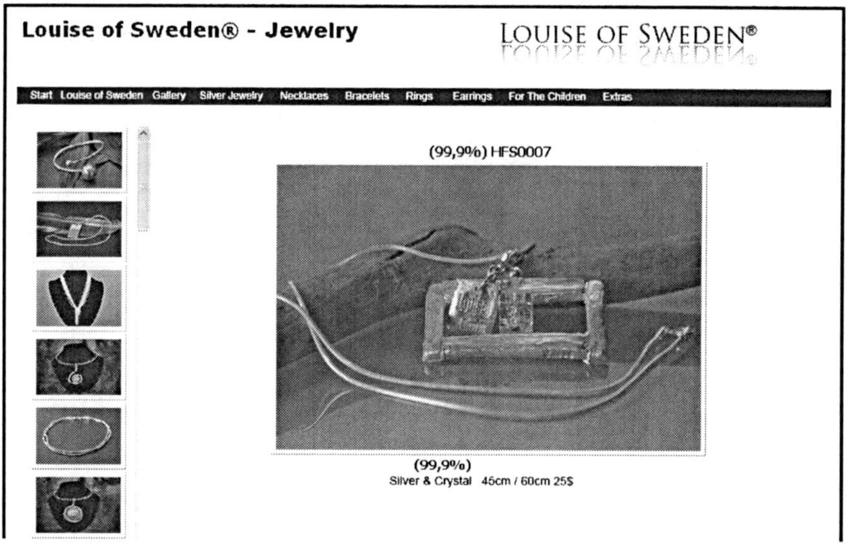


PICTURE 30. Louise of Sweden

The example shows that it's important for all types of websites to consider what the visitor is going to do. Louise of Sweden is a small company that sells and markets handmade jewellery. Like many other small companies, they use the website as the main, and perhaps only, source of marketing and sales. Louise of Sweden managed to attract visitors, but few bought the products. The website was done by Louise of Sweden on their own, and the creators are very familiar with the products and how a customer will find the purchase function. The problem was that the visitors weren't buying the products – and the cause had nothing to do with the look of the jewellery or the quality. Instead, it was that the website worked more as a display window than as a web shop where the products could be placed in a shopping cart. To buy something, the visitor had to go to "Contact" and once there, fill in an order form. Only a few visitors managed to figure that out. One solution was to create an actual web shop, but for Louise of Sweden, something needed to be done that worked with the existing website. The solution wasn't that difficult to find. It only took a few minutes to add a small function to each page:

PICTURE 31. Louise of Sweden with an Order Here button

A button with the text "Order here" was the simple solution. According to Louise of Sweden, the number of visitors that became customers rose sharply. The order-here button was a simple and obvious success.

## Content and Conversion – What the Visitor Wants

The first website was published in December 1990 by Tim Berners Lee who at the time worked for the Cern Research Institute in Switzerland. The address was (and is) www.cern.ch. Unfortunately, there are no copies or pictures of what the original website looked like, but the structure looked roughly like this:

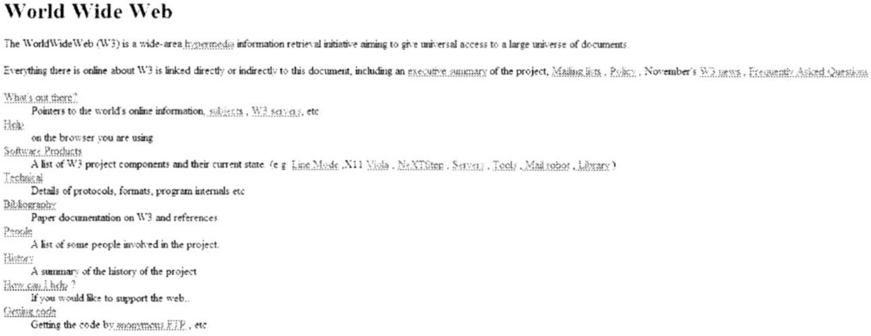

**World Wide Web**

The WorldWideWeb (W3) is a wide-area hypermedia information retrieval initiative aiming to give universal access to a large universe of documents.

Everything there is online about W3 is linked directly or indirectly to this document, including an executive summary of the project, Mailing lists , Policy , November's W3 news , Frequently Asked Questions .

What's out there?
Pointers to the world's online information, subjects , W3 servers, etc
Help
on the browser you are using
Software Products
A list of W3 project components and their current state. (e.g. Line Mode ,X11 Viola , NeXTStep , Servers , Tools , Mail robot , Library )
Technical
Details of protocols, formats, program internals etc
Bibliography
Paper documentation on W3 and references
People
A list of some people involved in the project.
History
A summary of the history of the project
How can I help ?
If you would like to support the web..
Getting code
Getting the code by anonymous FTP , etc

PICTURE 32. Example of an early website

It was a page of fairly simple character. But still, today's observer can see that it's a website because there are links. At that time, unvisited links were blue, and they changed to purple after a visit. The system is simple, and creates no doubt about which pages were opened. Pretty soon, the ability to code both text and images was developed so that a web browser could read them. That's why we quickly had websites that looked like this on the following page:

PICTURE 33. Design came to the web (?)

It was so easy to produce a website that anyone who had the desire and the opportunity went on the net and made history. However, the results were of varying quality.We can describe the development of the web through simple timeline:

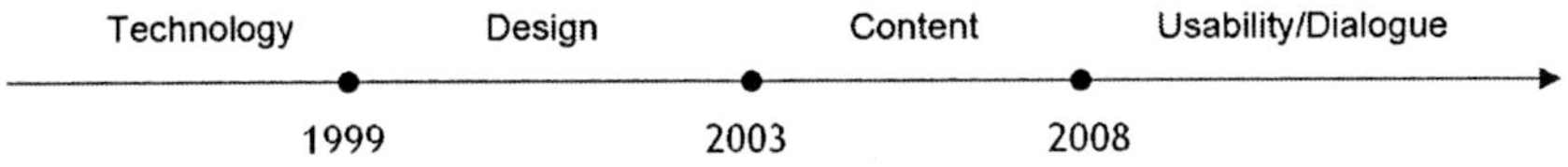


Up until 1999, technique was the driving force of the web. If a person knew the technique behind building a website, then that person got the job. From 1999 until 2003, the web was design-driven. Advertising agencies had their eyes opened to the web, and a lot of focus was on design. A lot of time was put into finding a website that stood out and was different. Text and image were dealt with in the same way as printed brochures. Experiments with navigation made it challenging to even understand how to manoeuvre on the website. It was then that the phrase "We don't read long texts on the web" was coined. This caused texts to be scaled down to short, and in some cases too short, texts. Research from the Poynter Institute in the US shows that we will gladly read long texts on the web as long as they're interesting and well written. So let's break the myth that short is better.After 2003, content started to take over. It was and is content that drives a website and generates visitors. It's the content that gets us to find new websites, and makes us return to a website we've already visited. Technique and design are obviously still important for all websites. Good technique and design make visitor-friendly navigation and focus on content. Since 2008, technique and design have contributed to a move towards more user-centred websites that communicate with the visitor. Usability is becoming all the more important, since we get tired of visiting complicated and hard-to-navigate websites. Navigation, searching and different spaces that guide the visitor are designed to work together on modern websites. The various preferences of the visitor demand individual options.The invitation to dialogue has been shown to be successful, even in such cases as the presidential election. Barack Obama and Hillary Clinton had a tough battle in the American primaries where they competed to be the presidential candidate for the Democratic Party. Both of them used the Internet as a platform for their campaigns. Clinton sent out information in the traditional "sender-recipient-variation" while Obama dialogued with his voters – a tactic that succeeded, and the rest is history.We also have lowered patience with websites where we have to think about the next step, where usability is poor, and we grow tired if we can't achieve the goal. Steven Krug sums this up quite well in the title of his book, "Don't Make Me Think.".

## Structure and Navigation Map

In section 1, we discussed the importance of top navigation. In reality, the entire navigation structure is of immense importance in our experience of a website. We want to understand and be able to choose the type of content that fits our needs at that particular moment. We want to understand what is in the menus, and not have to guess our way through by test clicking different menu choices to see what content is hiding behind the links. The entire menu system needs to be organized on the visitor's terms. Certain websites have different target groups with different knowledge bases. A website that is designed for end customers (novices) and experts needs to satisfy the needs of both groups. If the language is too technical, the naïve customer won't understand; if the language is too simple, the experts will lose faith, and consider the website frivolous. The top navigation needs to work for and take care of both target groups.The structure of the website needs to be carefully planned both in the start up phase, and in the day-to-day maintenance. Top navigation is usually fairly static, perhaps with occasional small changes. It's possible that certain options can be added to the top navigation, but the pre-study should have preferably found a top navigation that will last for a longer period of time. It's on the next level that changes usually occur. Each option in the top navigation often results in its own second level. Underneath the second level, there can exist a third level, and in some cases, even a fourth. In terms of structure, it's better to create a structure that has at most three levels, and to find other ways to handle more levels. The structural designer needs to understand that the texts in the menu should be descriptive, and easy to understand for the target groups. Neither should the menu texts be weighted wrong. This means that the menu rows on the same level need to be equally important; in other words, they need to have the same level of detail. An example of a wrongly weighted menu:

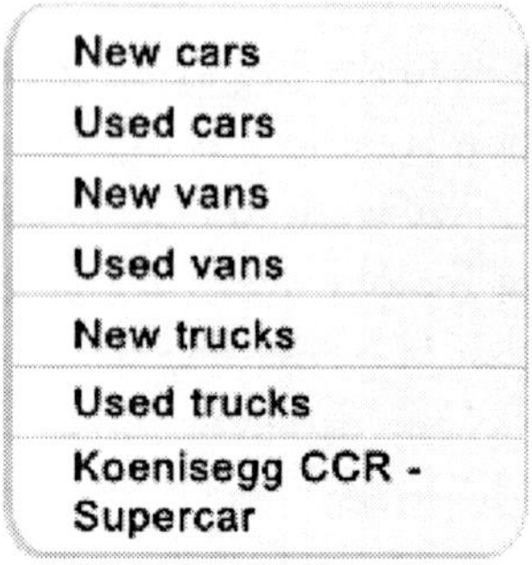


PICTURE 34. Example of a wrongly weighted menu

Here, the website wants to boast that they have a really nice and expensive car for sale. It can of course be a thought to separate it simply because of that, but structurally, it belongs under new cars or used cars. If the web editor wants to advertise that car, there are other ways to do it.

## Column for Converting and to Lead the Visitor Onward

We mentioned earlier that modern computers have wider screens that make it possible to divide a website's space into several parts. The width of the content section is limited by the ideal length of a row of text. The recommendation of 55-70 characters within typography also applies to websites. Any more characters and we have difficulties finding the beginning of the next row, any fewer and the text is deemed difficult to read. In other words, there is space for both a menu and a column beside the main text. We call the column the conversion column, and it should be used so that the visitor can achieve the various goals of the website. This is where the visitor can become a customer, receive special offers for extra sales, be shown relevant content or quite simply be inspired by images and other brand-building content.

## How does the Visitor Take the Next Step?

When a visitor comes to a website, she often discovers that she needs more information. This is when the links are a deciding factor. Many writers think that text for a web page can simply be lifted from printed material. We've already stressed the importance of writing for both the visitor and for search engines. An important text form on the web is links. Printed text in a brochure or a book doesn't have links – instead, you can flip between pages. On page four, a reader has the option of flipping ahead to page five, or back to page three. She can also go completely crazy and flip to page 12! The website's pages lack an inherent order, which means that a link doesn't mean moving "forward" or "backward." Instead, a link is a challenge to the visitor to do something. If the visitor is ready, she will click, otherwise she'll keep reading. A link can offer such things as:

- Find more details.
- Contact a seller or administrator.
- Buy now and save 10 percent.
- If you're interested in X, you might be interested in Y.
- Here's some related information.
- Apply for something on a public website.

Links in the text are some of the most important advantages of a website, compared to a brochure with similar content. Links let the visitors discover more content, and take the visitor further on the website. Although links are useful, the number of links on the content sections should be limited to one per paragraph. A maximum of three or four per page is also a good rule of thumb to avoid texts that are too hard to read.

## The Hidden Content

Earlier we talked about Louise of Sweden and how they hid the function to buy the products. A webmaster or web editor knows her own website inside and out. She knows the structure, what content is available, and how a visitor should behave to achieve the goals of the website. The problem is that she knows her website too well. A website always has hidden functions that are of great interest for a visitor, yet still hard to find. It could be delivery information for when a purchase has been made through a web shop, or shipping costs incurred with an order. On each page, therefore, perhaps you need to provide the visitor with more information than what is available where she is. It's not about jumping somewhere else with links; it could be enough with help text or other small functions that the visitor needs in order to move on in the website. An editor should always think about what a visitor on a certain page needs in addition to the obvious content.

## Different Types of Content

There are lots of different types of information on a website. The homepage should have a certain type of content. When we navigate further down in the structure, the content becomes more and more specific and rich in content. The content on a homepage can be angled in two different ways. If it's designed to take care of new visitors, then it should lead them to the appropriate section on the website. It could also be focused more on returning visitors and the homepage should then show new content. The latter option is applicable to newspaper or municipal websites, for example. The first option is more for organizations with more static content. These are two extremes, and there are naturally lots of websites that are a mixture of both. What is common between them is that they present the sender. Who is behind the website, and why does it exist? The parallels to the cover for a video are not far fetched. The cover should present the film with a bit of text and some images, convincing the person holding the video case to buy or rent the video. Another parallel that can be drawn is with a store. When a visitor comes into a store, she can quickly take a look around and get an idea of what the store has to offer. If the store is quite large, this becomes harder, but the parallel applies even here, since the same problem occurs on a large website. What should be visible to the visitor and what can be left out? The start page can be described as the website's outward image. The visitor should feel welcome and be able to have a quick scan. Top navigation and key words should offer attractive entry points to even more content. The homepage is still important, but remember that it is losing ground through visitors landing on other parts of the website. Web statistics from 2009 show that between 20 and 30 percent of visitors never see the homepage during the visit to the website[23]. This number has increased over the years since traffic from search engines, for example, has increased and often leads to traffic to a page lower down in the structure.When a visitor clicks further in the structure, she lands either on a content page or a secondary homepage. On larger websites, secondary homepages are common. It's a homepage for that section of the website, and a gathering area for the content that exists underneath it in the structure. Different target groups can be interested by different areas of the website, and it's quite possible that this is where a bookmark leads. It's also becoming commonplace that organizations communicate not just their domain name, but also the domain name followed by a catalogue name, so that the visitor will be led directly to the secondary homepage.Under the homepages, there are content pages. One trick is to put pages that contain lots of specific information lower down in the structure, while those pages that contain less complex information are placed earlier. The idea behind this is that a visitor will first have an

23 Statistics are taken from ca. 50 websites that are analyzed monthly by Two (two.se)

overview, and then gain more and weightier information. The pages with more, and more specific, information are often the ones that rank well, since search engines like lots of text. It also makes us as visitors keep clicking, as long as the trail is hot, until we find the information we're looking for.Images are a way to lighten the information. Studies that examine eye tracking show that the eye is drawn towards images, regardless of whether they are in newspapers or on a website. Good images that complement and simplify the content can spur a visitor on in their search for the goal.

## Step-by-step Guides

On a website, there is often a need to create a guide or a step-by-step process that will take the visitor through the website in a certain way. The most common is the process of purchasing on a web shop, or via a booking routine on a tourism website. There are other areas where such guides can be used. All forms of education or knowledge transfer lend themselves to be structured into steps. A visitor will start a guide to learn something, and she always knows where in the process she is, and what remains to be done. In other words, it's important to show how many steps are left, and which steps have been completed. It should be possible to move backwards in the guide, as well as forward. In certain instances, a guide can be binding. Such an example would be purchasing or booking something. In these cases, a binding guide can lead to more purchases. At the same time, it's important that the visitor doesn't feel forced into buying something, which could make them cancel the purchase.Guides can be set up on different levels according to knowledge base, and it is a finesse to lead the visitor to a purchase or a contact during the process. You can have steps where the visitor learns things through text, images, sound or video. A good idea is to use a section of a form for visitors to tell about their requirements, and in a later step send in that information, or print it to have with them when they visit an actual store to buy the product. A good example of this is with vehicle manufacturers or vehicle agents, where there are guides for building a car. The visitor can, step by step, build her own car and at the end of the guide, she has the option to send it in to a retailer or to print it to take with her to a salesperson. The work that was previously done at the sales desk has now been done by the visitor herself. The list of options has also been decided before the physical meeting at the car dealership, where certain makes and models have been left out. The meeting now focuses on details and discussions about prices. If the salesperson is competent, she can perhaps sell a more expensive car, but oftentimes the visitor has already decided what she wants. Booking a test drive, building a car, and booking a service time are examples of services that end up on the website and make life easier for the organization. Those car dealerships that keep up with developments will have more business, since their customers consider it a given that such functions should exist.

## The Appearance of Links and Backgrounds

One of the biggest challenges for all websites is to make things easy for the visitor. The visitor shouldn't have to stop and think about what will happen in the next step. It's about the sum of the parts, rather than the large structures, making a website better than the competitor's. It could be as simple as the colour scheme and what the links look like. The design will often remain unchanged during the website's life span or until the organization reworks their graphic profile. One way to start experimenting a little bit is to test small variations in the interface. It's possible to work with the look of the links, the background colours, and the colour of the list of links, as well as testing different placements, colours and functions in forms. All changes should be able to be analyzed with the statistics tool, or in some other form of analysis tool. The goal is that more visitors will achieve any one of the website's goals. Does a red button work better than a blue one? Maybe it shouldn't be a button at all, but a link with a picture instead that will take the visitor further?It could be good for the organization's business to show one variation to a certain number of visitors, and another variation to others, to see which version works best. The correct term for testing appearance and function is A/B testing[24]. More than two variations can be tested – that depends on the number of visitors. "Multivariate testing" is when more than two variations are tested at the same time, but works in the same way. Two different versions are a good starting point, after which more options can be tested against the winning version. Sometimes, extremely small details make a large difference. On a larger poker site, it was shown that considerably more visitors clicked further in to the poker rooms when the links in the top-ten list were underlined compared to if they weren't. The background colour also influenced a visitor's willingness to click.It's all about fine-tuning, and thereby gaining more customers. In the end, it all comes down to money. Think about what would happen if a red button increases sales by 15 000 dollars, compared to a blue button that was chosen because it fit so well with the design.

## Structured Work with Content

In certain cases, it can be difficult in an organization to identify who is responsible for the website's content. This depends of course on the size of the organization, and how well developed the website is. But it's often hard to place the website in relation to marketing efforts and other tasks that take care of customers. A worthwhile comparison is to place the web visits in relation to telephone contact and physical meetings. Place the numbers into the following equations:

24 A/B testing is a version of a test where two different options are compared to see which is most effective. If there are more than two options, the test is called "multivariate testing"

- Divide the number of daily calls to the switchboard with the number of full-time positions needed to respond.
- Divide the number of visitors that walk through the organization's front door every day with the number of positions allocated to sitting at the reception desk.
- Divide the number of visits to the website each day with the number of positions need to manage and update the website.

The results of the equations almost always show that there are more staff taking care of phone calls and "real" visitors than managing the website. Those visitors that visit the website are less visible, even though this is often the figure that is brought forward in the web statistics. To be able to work structurally with the content, the website needs to be given the space it deserves in an organization.

## How Important is the Website?

Public speaker and author Fredrik Härén often talks about how the web increases the chances for all kinds of niche interests to develop. His example is usually about "hats for dogs." Up until 1995, the hats-for-dogs-industry had a rather obscure existence. Let's say that, in 1993, someone in northern England was interested in hats for dogs. How did this person find someone who shared her interest? If the city had maybe 100 000 inhabitants, there must be at least one like-minded person. In 1993, bulletin boards in grocery stores and newspapers the only ways to look for contacts. After placing an ad in one of the city's newspapers, there was a message on the answering machine. The person on the other line was also interested in hats for dogs, and the two people decided to sit down at a pub to talk. They discovered that there was a catalogue in the US (of course) that dealt only with hats for dogs. It took six weeks before the catalogue came to the northern

English city, and it didn't take long for the catalogue to become torn to shreds from use, in the hunt for the perfect hats.Check out a search engine today and search for "hat for dog." See how many pages are indexed, i.e. how many hits you get. Has the hats-for-dogs-industry grown faster today than it did in 1993? Via newsletters, forums and web shops, the entire hats-for-dogs-industry has control over all the products that are produced all over the world. Information published in Japan is available in Sweden only a few seconds after it was first made public on the other side of the world. It is very likely that the hats-for-dogs-industry is developing considerably faster today than it did in 1993.The Internet and the web have had considerable influence for all industries, and it's therefore a good idea to think about who is going to work structurally with the organization's website. Who is it that will make sure that a visitor is taken care of and supported on her way to becoming a customer?

# Summary of Taking Care of Visitors and Turning them into Customers

To be able to take care of customers, a website needs to have concrete and well-defined goals. Those goals should in some way be measurable and analyzable. The organization needs to know that the right visitor is attracted to the website and that she can clearly reach what she strives for. A visitor will happily click around on the website as long as her interest is maintained. When the trail goes cold, it doesn't take long to leave the website and search somewhere else. That's why it's always important to look at how a visitor navigates and how the content and functionality answer the visitor's demands and wishes. A website that takes care of the customer and gives her what she wants has a great advantage over the competition.A web editor needs to have the ability to see the website from a visitor perspective. This is one of the hardest things to do. That's why it's important to go over the statistics regularly and to see how your website is performing and how a visitor experiences the website.

# *Section 4.* Analyzing the Website to Increase Business Value

Compared to other media, the Internet is almost 100 percent measureable. The website also offers the possibility to measure the effects of other types of marketing efforts. Statistics tools are quite effective because they analyze in real time how the website performs. Sadly, most people content themselves with just looking at the number of visitors the website has. In section 1, we talked about what was best from a visitor perspective, 10 or 100 000 visitors, and decided that it depends on what a visitor does on the website. Marketing and sales departments often want to measure the results of various marketing efforts. Even though it is entirely possible to do that, few organizations take the initiative for web analysis, and may not even have someone responsible to analyze and follow up with what happens on the website.

Analyzing a website with the help of statistics demands constant attention, where the web analyst looks at how the website lives up to the established goals, and suggests improvements.

of work happens in three stages:

1. t data
2. analyze
3. make appropriate improvements.

Sometimes, making small changes, such as clarifying a button or a link, can make large improvements; sometimes it's a question of carrying out larger structural changes to lead the visitor to the right content. The web statistics are the basis for a website that performs well.

## Using Statistics Tools to Analyze Goals

For web analysis, you can presuppose four models. Some websites can have all four models, but it's usually enough to create segments in the statistics tool in order to have good structure and measurability. The different models are:

- Web shop or booking system: for example amazon.com, where you can buy books. The object of this model is to sell lots and to have the visitor come back often and buy more.
- Content and advertising: the visitor should come back often and preferably see many pages during each visit. An example is nytimes.com or thestar.com.
- Collect customer leads: have visitors submit contact information so the organization has a prospect to work with. An example is two.se.
- Customer support: the goal is to provide the best service and information to support customers and potential customers, and to reduce telephone support. An example is t-mobile.com.

We've already talked about the importance of establishing goals for a website and to make them measurable. The art of analyzing and measuring the goals can be summed up in a few simple points:

1. Choose goals and potential secondary goals.
2. Decide how they will be measured.
3. Set up the statistics tool to measure the goals.
4. Monitor the goals and analyze the results.
5. Make changes.

Steps four and five occur constantly, and are part of a continuous process. Sometimes new goals are added, and sometimes other goals can be dismantled.

The Key Performance Indicators (KPI) need to be translatable, i.e. you need to be able to decide which results are acceptable and which ones need work. It's important to decide what an acceptable increase is, or how low the value is allowed to go before measures are taken.

## Measurable Goals

What is considered a good or poor measured value depends on the website's aims. For example, what is a good value when you measure the number of pages visited per visit: one, three, five or seven? If we're talking about a newspaper website that sells banner ad, five can be okay, but two quite poor, since we want as much exposure as possible for banners. For a website where the visitor needs to find a telephone number, two is a good value. A visitor's goal is to find the number quickly: on the first page, the question is asked; on the second page the answer is given, if everything works the way it should. If the visitor doesn't find the right number, she will search again, which will increase the number of pages viewed, which is not optimal. The goal for the website should be that everyone can find what they're looking for as quickly as possible.

A good base model is to try to improve the quality, or value, of each visit, instead of maximizing the number of visitors at any cost. This is usually easier and cheaper in the long run since it requires optimizing the website, rather than paying for expensive campaigns and other marketing strategies. It's only when you're happy with the measured value for each visitor that you can look at how to attract more visitors. Sometimes, time constraints and other external occurrences can cause problems for this kind of work, in which case the two models (i.e. improving quality and expensive campaigns) can be used simultaneously.

It's hard to know what is a good value for a goal. A web analyst or a web strategist often has more information to offer, and it's always a good idea to ask for help in questions of measuring value. It's about finding relevant and appropriate goals for the organization, goals that are easy to analyze and that the internal staff can understand and relate to.

When the goals are formulated, and the various limits established, you simply have to retrieve the values from the statistics tool. In relation to this work, dashboards are valuable – pages where there are different scales that show how the website is doing. Additionally, it's possible to get personalized statistics reports for the different internal target groups. You also have to decide how often the values will be measured and analyzed. This is a question of how much the organization will lose if the time intervals are too large. It's no good if the results of a sponsored link campaign are analyzed three weeks after the campaign if something had gone wrong – by then it's too late. The analysis needs to be adjusted in time for the measured value, and with regards to how important it is for turnover and profit for the organization.

There are also measurable goals that don't exactly provide a value for the organization but that indicate what content is popular or not. Using statistics, you can see which pages are viewed most, as well as see what content prompted the visitor to make a decision and act in some way. An example of this is a standard collection of products on a website. You can see which product pages are most popular. A top-ten list can be interesting from an analysis perspective. Sometimes, downloadable files with more detailed information can be added to a product. The statistics about how often such files are downloaded can also give an indication of how interested the visitor is in different products.

Sound, film and other types of moving content are becoming more and more common. It's interesting to know how long a visitor has watched a film, or how far in the flash-graphic a visitor has navigated. With a decent statistics tool, you can dictate that a visitor will see at least X minutes of a film. If it becomes obvious that the content isn't being shown to the extent needed to justify production costs, think about the reason for this. It could be that the visitor can't find the film, or that the material doesn't fit the content, or that it's quite simply not good enough.

## Interested Parties of Web Analysis

The results of web analysis are relevant for different interest groups within the organization – from the CEO to individuals with different areas of responsibility. An IT-department that develops the website is interested in the technical values such as the choice of platform (computer, cell phone etc) or whether the visitor can use JavaScript. A marketing department wants to know how the different marketing plans have gone, and a sales organization wants to know more about the sales related areas. A web editor is interested in the kinds of content a visitor looks at, and which parts aren't visited at all. The one responsible for search engines focuses on which search engines create traffic, and which search words have generated that traffic. There are many target groups and it can be worthwhile to give everyone access to the statistics tool with their own dashboards, reports and KPI's. With the right knowledge, it's much easier to implement appropriate measures, which will give the website even more business value. The problem with trying to lump everyone together into one dashboard, or one report that all interested parties get, is the report is too general and doesn't help anyone. A good metaphor is the Swiss Army knife. It's easy to carry with you, but the individual components are inferior to using a proper tool. The general report is easy to create and circulate, but not as usable as a smaller report designed for individual target groups. Of course, the web master should always strive to have comprehensive knowledge of all measured values to be able to have an overall picture.

## Determining the Value of a Visit

In many cases, it's possible to place value or worth on a visit to a website. This, of course, depends on the type of website we're talking about, and it's usually easiest for a web shop or a website where you can book something. Business is conducted right on the website, and you can figure out the average purchase value and relate it to the number of visitors. Let's take a simple example of a website that collects customer contact, i.e. prospects.

The website has 4 000 unique visitors per month. Of these 4 000, 20 fill in a contact form and the organization has a prospective customer they can work with. Of the 20 contacts, an average of five will lead to an order worth 30 000 dollars. The total order value is five times 30 000 dollars, which is 150 000 dollars. The value of the prospective customer is then 150 000 divided by 20 = 7 500 dollars. Spread across all visitors, that comes to 37.50 dollars per visitor (150 000/4 000). If we double the number of visitors (meaning visitors of the same type), it is reasonable to assume that we will generate business for an additional 150 000 dollars. Based on these figures, it's easy to calculate how much a recruiting effort (attracting more visitors to the website) can cost and still be profitable. Regardless of the type of website, the above numbers can be calculated. In cases involving support webs, it's possible to calculate money saved; in other cases, it's possible to calculate profits. With regards to support webs, the calculation is based on the web solving problems for customers, which results in the customer support department being able to get by with fewer staff. Non-profit organizations can calculate saved time, since visitors can read and execute services on the website that otherwise would have required staff. With a value placed on a visitor, it's much easier to see which marketing strategies will work and stay within budget, and which ones won't.

## What is Web Analysis?

Web statistics are generated by a statistics tool whose object is to measure the website. The definition of web analysis, according to Web Analytics Association in the US is "the measurement, collection, analysis and reporting of Internet data for the purposes of understanding and optimizing Web usage."

Besides statistics tools and the classic stance on web analysis, there are other ways to measure a website. When an organization does long-term work on a website, and has as a goal to achieve a high ranking in a search engine, it's possible to work with so-called ranking reports that show the results of different words and how they get placed in the results list. We've also mentioned earlier a method to test the website called eye tracking. This means that a certain number of people get to test the website and the results show how and in what order the different objects were read. Finally, there are always different sorts of interviews and question-based research that can provide valuable information about what visitors think is good or not, as well as what type of content should be added. The analysis of all of these sources provides a good base for a web analyst to be able to better understand the activities and visitors of a website.

Everything on a website can be measured, provided all measuring tools are in place and properly installed, and that the organization realizes the value of continuous work with results analysis. There is tremendous business value in analyzing the website. Through analysis, there is a lot to be learned about how a website performs, and how it can be changed to be better and to save or earn money for the organization. A simple function is that all statistics tools, even those that are free, measure the traffic generated by other websites. The next time a salesperson calls and wants to extend an advertisement or a link in a catalogue, you can see in the statistics tool if the advertisement has been profitable in terms of number of visitors. In more advanced tools, it's possible to see how many of these visitors have accomplished a goal, and which one. Everything is there in black and white, and can be positioned in relation to the cost of the advertisement. It's suddenly possible to measure the results of different marketing strategies. John Wanamaker, founder of "Wanamaker's Department Stores" is seen as the father of modern advertising. Wanamaker was the first businessman who hired his own copywriter in 1880. One of his most famous quotes was "Half the money I spend on advertising is wasted; the trouble is, I don't know which half." With web statistics and web analysis, we can now filter out those parts that aren't profitable.

What follows below is a discussion of the direct effects in terms of measurability and goal achievement of campaigns in relation to analysis. The long-term effects of marketing in terms of brand name perception and other brand name building measures are not dealt with in this book. We deal strictly with following up on business transactions, and measuring the results of what the campaigns and the website provide from a strategic business perspective.

## Free or Paid Tools

There are both free and paid tools for gathering web statistics. Since there are quite large differences between the various tools, it's good to do a needs-analysis before an organization chooses a tool. There are reasons why one tool is free and one costs money. They are not in the same class with regards to function. It isn't the size of the organization that should decide the tool, but the need. A small web shop can earn lots of money by purchasing a more expensive and competent tool, since the profit gained by using that tool is much greater than the cost savings they could achieve by using a free tool. A paid tool also has better functions for analyzing the flows and follow-ups than a free tool has. You might think that they would all measure in the same way, but that's not the case. There are different ways to collect the measured values, and, as a general rule, the tools that cost money have better ways to collect those values, which makes them more exact. The choice of statistics tool is sort of like buying your first espresso machine (or any other kind of machine where the buyer is ignorant of quality and function). After having read up a little bit, 15-bar pumps, good steam and other important functions become comprehensible. The first choice is usually based more on economy than need. It's often a fairly simple machine that won't hold up in the long run. The trick is to weigh all issues, and really examine the needs, otherwise you may end up with a machine that takes forever to make three cups of poor-tasting coffee for your dinner guests.

If price is the leading factor influencing the choice, then it's still better to use a free tool, rather than not measuring the web at all. That is the first step, but it's important to still be aware of the limits a free tool could place on the analysis. A powerful tool with the ability to see the big picture can be considered expensive in the short term. However, it's important to look beyond the price tag and consider the long-term profits.

## The Fundamentals of Statistics Tools

To understand the numbers and data a statistics tool generates, it's beneficial to be familiar with a number of terms and concepts. In the previous section, we mentioned that different statistics tools can measure in different ways. It's all about how a tool collects the measured values, i.e. the data from a visit from a web browser. What is normally considered a visitor is actually a unique web browser, not an actual person. A connection is made to the statistics company's server and the measuring takes place as soon as a page is completely loaded. This is done by a few rows of statistics code in the website's html code. There are two options for placement. The statistics counter can be first or last in the html code, i.e. the code that builds the website. The advantage to using the first option is that the statistics counter starts as soon as a page starts loading for a visitor. The downside is that it doesn't analyze whether the entire page was loaded and shown to the visitor. If the visitor has a slow connection, there is a risk that the page didn't finish loading before the visitor closed the web browser or clicked back or forward. It has therefore been counted that a visitor has seen the page, even though she may not have.

The other option is that the statistics code is at the bottom of the page. It is activated only when the entire page has loaded and is visible to the visitor. The advantage here is that it is guaranteed that the visitor has seen the page before the statistics code connects. However, the downside is that a quick visitor can click on a link before the page has loaded completely, and the visit doesn't have time to get registered.

The golden median is to put the statistics code in the middle of the page. This brings with it, however, the same disadvantage as with option one (at the beginning of the page), plus the fact that it's never a good idea to put too much code in the middle of a page. There are web browsers for the blind, and search engine spiders that don't like JavaScript code in the middle of the page's html code.

The best solution, therefore, is to put it at the end of the page. If the page takes a very long time to load, and the visitor clicks her way off the website before the statistics code is loaded, then the problem isn't with the placement of the code, but rather with the slow loading time. The code will pose the least problems there, and will connect first when the page is loaded, which is good for the web analyst who can be sure that all page views are correct.

There are a number of statistics tools that are very specialized in their functions, where the ultimate goal is to show which organization is visiting the website. This is not about knowing who it is, but within which organization the individual works.

## Visitors and Visits

A visitor can be new or returning. This is measured with the help of a so-called "cookie". A cookie is a small text file that lands on a visitor's computer and is contacted by the statistics tool for verification every time a visitor comes to a website.

This is when we get to one of the larger differences between various statistics tools and also how a statistics tool can be set up. A cookie can be defined in two different ways. It can be defined as a first party cookie or a so-called third party cookie. There is no such thing as a second party cookie, because the names don't reference an ordering, but rather a relationship between different parties where the third party is separated from the two parties that have a relationship. First party cookies are the best, since they likely have solid control over who is a new visitor and who is a returning visitor. The third party variation is not very good at being able to distinguish a new visitor and a returning one. It's often the free tools that have third party cookies, or at least a poorly implemented solution for first part cookies, while the paid tools have the option of using first party cookies. There are exceptions to this, but more and more web analysts are aware of the problem and make sure to use first party cookies. The largest difference between the two types of cookies is that, with a first party cookie, it's the domain name in the visitor's web browser that places the "mark of recognition" on her computer. With regards to third party cookies, it's the statistics company's domain name that places the cookie. In other words, the domain name that places the cookie and the domain name shown in the web browser are not the same. The cookie is placed by a third party, i.e. the statistics company's domain name. In the free tools segment there are tools that actually set a first part cookie but via a JavaScript. A visitor who has turned off JavaScript is not counted at all!

This is complicated, but it's worth noting, since the measured value that comes in needs to be as precise as possible. Third party cookies are problematic, because many security companies filter them and the cookie never lands on the visitor's computer. Such a visitor will then always be seen as a new visitor. The result is that the numbers for new vs. returning visitors will be different depending on if you use first or third party cookies. Unfortunately, there are no decent standards for how we measure a website, and different analysis tools can provide different results.

There is a difference between a visit and a visitor. A visitor can visit a website several times a day. She is still a unique visitor who has made numerous visits. A visit will "time out" (be considered as finished" after 20-30 minutes of inactivity on the website. Here is an example: Charlie is sitting in his office at work and begins his morning by visiting a website. After a while, he takes a coffee break and leaves the website and closes his browser. After 15 minutes, he comes back and opens the website again and continues his visit. Since Charlie was inactive for less than 30 minutes, he is considered the same visitor on the same visit.

Another example: Charlie is on the same website right before lunch and is navigating his way around. Lisa pops in and says they need to hurry for lunch. Charlie forgets to close his web browser. After 40 minutes, he comes back from lunch and picks up surfing where he left off. Charlie is now on a new visit, even though he didn't close his web browser. But he is still the same visitor he was in the morning. He has made two visits to the website, and is one visitor.

## Page Views

Page views measure the number of pages that have been shown under a certain period of time. Some older statistics tools use the word hits, which is something quite different. According to the hit-method, if a page has three images it will count as four hits, but still only one page view. Page views can be connected to visitors, which makes it possible to figure out the number of page views per visit or per unique visitor. It's also possible to see which pages different visitors have navigated through during their visits, and navigation between two pages counts each new viewing of the page as a page view. Even when the visitor updates her web browser via the refresh button, it counts as a new page view.

It's important not to confuse a page view with a visit, which is an easy mistake.

## Sources of Traffic

For a web analyst, it's important to know where a visitor comes from. A visit can come from another website that isn't a search engine, a so-called referrer website. There is a variation of a referrer website, which is a referral through redirect. This means that an advertisement is placed on a website, but that it is managed by an advertising network. In this case, the visit comes from the advertising network.

The visit can come from a search engine, and here it's even possible to see which keywords the visitor searched for to come to the website, as well as if the visitor is coming from a paid or unpaid link. Finally, we have those visitors that type the domain name right in their browser (type ins), or have the website as a favourite or bookmark in the web browser.

## Segmentation

In many cases, the web analyst wants to see different types of visitors using one kind of statistics material. The option to filter out certain types of target groups is called segmentation. For example, it could be interesting to choose the visitors that, during a certain time period, have come from a search engine, or to see only those visitors that are from a specific country, or that have searched for a specific word. You can also segment out successful visits, i.e. visitors that have accomplished a goal of the website, which is very helpful in identifying patterns for successful visits. In most statistics tools (even the free ones), you can create a segment for different needs. Segmentation is of great help when evaluating marketing campaigns. It is possible to discount the visitors that didn't come from the current campaign, which allows the web analyst to see the various paths the visitors have taken from the campaign, as well as which visitors have achieved a goal, and other interesting measurable values.

## Bounce Rate

Bounce rate is a measurement for how many visitors leave a website at a certain stage. The analysis can, for example, examine how many people leave the website within five seconds, or after having looked at only one page. Another usable variation is to measure how many people disappear in each step (abandon rate). Bounce rate is one of the most important measures on a web site because it tells you what pages a visitor lands on and then directly disappears from. On a page with phone numbers, this could be a good thing but on a product page on a web shop it is not so good.

## Conversion Funnel

A conversion funnel is a way to measure a pre-determined flow on a website. It can be easiest compared to the steps in a purchase process on a web shop, or the process of booking a trip on a travel website. The measurement shows how many have visited the web shop, how many have added a product to the shopping cart, how many have proceeded to the checkout, gone to the payment page and finally how many have completed a purchase. In the statistics tool, the function is called a funnel because of the narrowing shape that shows how many visitors disappear in each step:

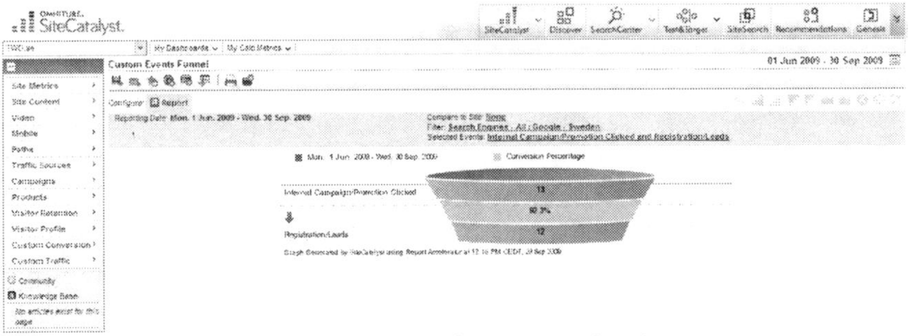


PICTURE 35. Example of a conversion funnel

## Dashboard

We've already gone over how a dashboard is a place that gathers all of the important measured values for a website and presents them in a clear and structured way. There should be different dashboards for different target groups within the organization. The marketing department and the information department are likely to be interested in different measured values, which means that their dashboards should look different. A dashboard should quickly show how the website is performing, and it should be a daily tool for analysis and management. A dashboard can also be suitable to present to the organization as a whole. It gives the employees an idea of how many people are on the website right now, how many have achieved the goals, and maybe even how many have landed on the website through a search engine. In this way, the employees have a feeling that the visitors on the website actually exist, and are worth as much as the people that call or visit the organization in reality. A dashboard can be set up in different ways with many general or fewer specific measured values. Here is one example:

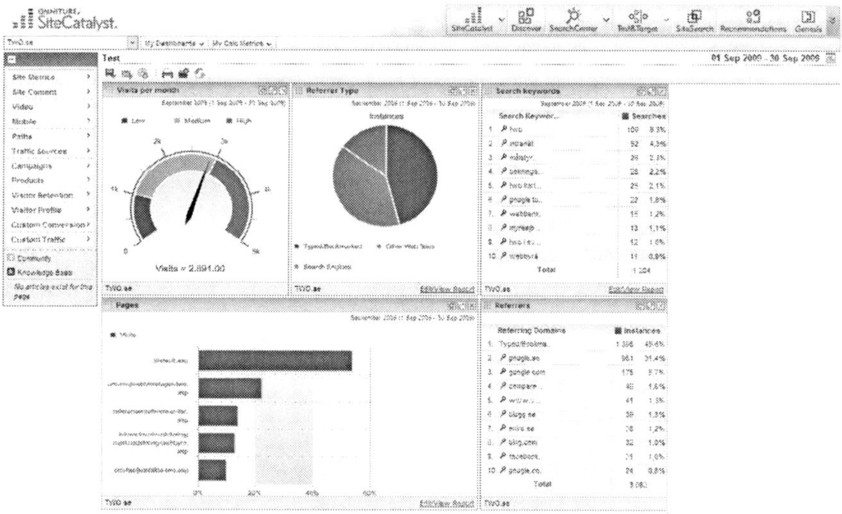


PICTURE 36. Example of a dashboard

## Groups of Measured Data

There are different types of measured data in a statistics there are basic data such as:

- visitors
- visits
- page views
- which pages are visited
- which parts of the content are most and least visited
- average visit length
- number of page visits

Then there is more technical information, such as:

- what web browser the visitor is using
- if JavaScript is enabled
- screen size
- the computer's platform (Mac, PC, or a mobile platform), etc.

## Use Statistics Tools to Analyze all Marketing

All marketing that is performed on the web is relatively easy to analyze with the website's statistics tool. However, it does take a lot of preparation to measure a banner campaign or sponsored links. Depending on the type of statistics tool the website uses, this could happen in a number of ways. Simpler (often free) tools require that there is a unique landing page for web traffic generated by the campaign. In order for the statistics tool to be able to report information about the number of visitors and their activity, the page can only be used for the campaign.

A more advanced tool is, of course, not free, but it gives more (and more advanced) opportunities to measure the campaign. For example, it's possible to "tag" those search paths that are connected to the campaign's banners and links. In this way, the tool knows that a specific visitor on the website has just come from that campaign.

The person responsible for the campaign can then segment the visitors and see what visitors from a certain campaign have done and if the campaign has achieved the right goals and given a good result. Several campaigns can run simultaneously and be analyzed both during and after they are finished.

### Analyze Campaigns Outside the Web

In theory, you can track and measure advertisements in media other than the web, for example TV, radio, newspapers and other types of printed ads. This is about sending out a message after which the receiver can take action via the website. Unique web addresses or campaign-specific domain names are two ways to measure such results.

An example would be an organization placing an advertisement in two separate magazines. In the first magazine, the reader can visit webstrategyfundamentals.com/job, and in the other magazine, the reader can visit webstrategyfundamentals.com/work. The web analys then creates two addresses so that the statistics can be calculated for each entry, and, according to the statistics tool's calculations, both addresses land on the same page on the website. Segmentation can then be used to see which magazine gave the best results. This technique can be used for all types of media outside the Internet. There is a certain margin of error for those visitors who don't type in the entire address, but simply type in the domain name. There are so many websites these days that have this form, which is why it's more common for a visitor to go directly to the right place, rather than finding her own way. This is most applicable to larger websites with lots of pages and different types of information.

You can also use temporary domain names for a specific campaign. This is clearer, and doesn't give anyone a choice in how the address will be given. Statistically, the procedure is the same; the difference lies in that the domain name needs to send someone to a landing page on the actual website.

A traditional way to do this is to use "coupons" that show that a visitor has seen a specific campaign. In this case, the coupon is some form of code that is used when the visitor comes to the website to complete the actions set out in the advertisement.

## Ranking Reports – How do you Place in Search Engines?

In the continuous task of improving a website's visibility in search engines, ranking reports are common. They are a good way to easily analyze and verify where important words and phrases end up in different search engines. At the same time, it's possible to analyze how well the competition is doing. The work is performed continuously with regular checkpoints, such as monthly, to prevent anything happening in the ranking result. With the report, you can also see which words have emerged, i.e. which words have ended up among the top arch engine. It's really no use to look beyond the first ry few visitors click further than that. You can also s have moved up, or improved their ranking, or if there s that have lost their position, i.e. decreased in ranking. With he help of a ranking report, the one responsible for search engines has a good overview of how well the work with website positioning is going. There is also the option of choosing different search engines to get an idea of whether the results for the same word differ between search engines.

With the help of the ranking report, the web editor and the person responsible for the search engine have a good base that shows which words need help. It also provides a guide over whether there needs to be links to a page with a specially chosen keyword in the link. Additionally, the report, together with the search engine statistics, gives an idea of which search engines are important to achieve a high ranking in. There are a number of search engines to choose between, and there can be quite distinctive differences between them in terms of searched words and phrases. Here's an example of a ranking report:

| Keywords | | Position | Prev | Change | Page | Best |
|---|---|---|---|---|---|---|
| keyword 1 | (125 000) | 1 | 1 | — | 1 | 1 |
| keyword 2 | (103 000) | 1 | 1 | — | 1 | 1 |
| keyword 3 | (113 000) | 2 | 2 | — | 1 | 2 |
| keyword 4 | (294 000) | 2 | 2 | — | 1 | 2 |
| keyword 5 | (56 100) | 4 | 5 | ▲ 1 | 1 | 4 |
| keyword 6 | (3 190 000) | 2 | 2 | — | 1 | 2 |
| keyword 7 | (859 000) | 2 | 2 | — | 1 | 2 |
| keyword 8 | (10 200) | 3 | 4 | ▲ 1 | 1 | 3 |
| keyword 9 | (245 000) | 2 | 3 | ▲ 1 | 1 | 2 |
| keyword 10 | (110 000) | 1 | 2 | ▲ 1 | 1 | 1 |
| keyword 11 | (53 800) | 1 | 1 | — | 1 | 1 |
| keyword 12 | (30 700) | 1 | 1 | — | 1 | 1 |
| keyword 13 | (21 700) | 3 | 4 | ▲ 1 | 1 | 3 |
| keyword 14 | (24 300) | 7 | 5 | ▼ 2 | 1 | 5 |
| keyword 15 | (44 900) | 9 | - | [+] | 1 | 9 |

| | | |
|---|---|---|
| — Not found | [+] Added | [x] Dropped |
| ▲ Moved Up | ▼ Moved Down | — Not Changed |

PICTURE 37. Example of a ranking report

# User Tests – How Visitors Use a Website

There are several ways to test how well a website is built. Aside from interviews, focus groups and tests with single users, there exists the possibility to gain a deeper understanding of the website and the visitors' motion patterns. First and foremost, there are tests that deal with eye tracking. With eye tracking, it's possible to see what a visitor has looked at during a visit to a website. The tester has several people perform tasks during a dialogue, and the conversation can be recorded on film or only with audio. Then, you can go back in the material and hear what the person says and connect it with what she does. The test can be task-based or free form, depending on what the test is trying to achieve. When a certain number of people have performed the test, the results are collated in different reports. Here are a couple of examples of reports:

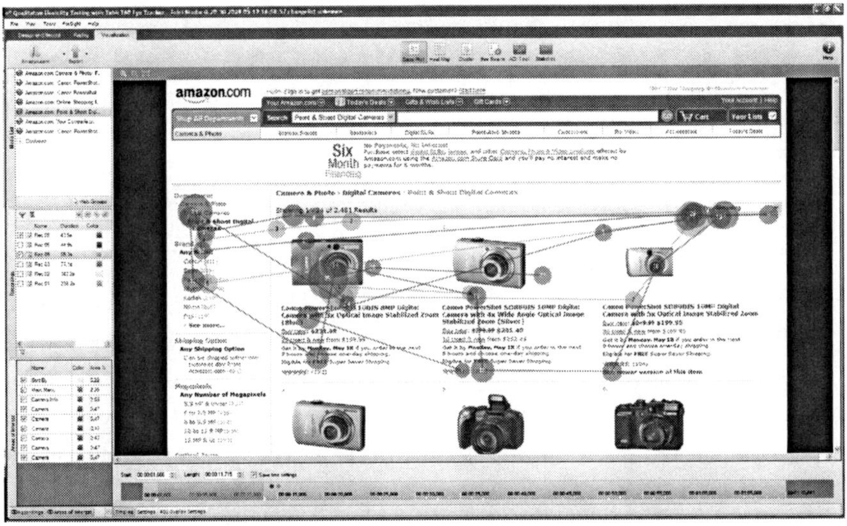


PICTURE 38. A so-called Gaze Plot from Tobii eye tracking: the picture shows the path that a visitor's gaze has taken over the picture.

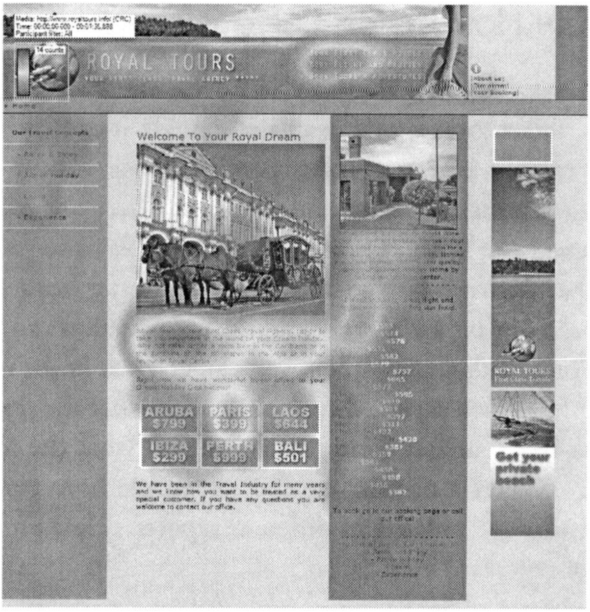


PICTURE 39. A so-called heat map from Tobii eye tracking: the picture shows where people have looked on the page. A darker area shows that more people have looked at those areas.

Together, interviews and mapping of where a visitor looks generate valuable information. It often becomes clear that what the person says doesn't always match with where the person looks. The person may claim not to have seen a certain piece of information, while the eye movements clearly show that she has looked at the part of the page where the information is. It's also possible to determine if the person is reading, or simply moving the eye over an area. Eye tracking is a common analysis method in both the US and Great Britain. With lower equipment costs and more analysts becoming aware of the technology, eye tracking will become more common in other areas of the world.

## Website Research

There are a number of options for conducting research on the actual website. This can include forms that pop up and ask the visitor to complete a task, usually involving answering a few questions. The problem is that it's difficult to know if the right target group has answered. Those that the organization wants to reach are perhaps experienced Internet users who get irritated by a form disrupting their visit. On well-visited websites with a wide target group, such research with well-chosen questions can be beneficial, but it's probably better to use other types of marketing research.

## Summary of Analysing the Website to Increase Business Value

Not using and analyzing web statistics is like driving a car in France without a map and GPS. The possibilities exist to achieve the goals, but the path may be crooked, long, and lead nowhere. Instead, use the web statistics as your map, and make use of a knowledgeable map-reader: the web analyst. In the next step, with the use of a GPS, you can learn how to find the fastest or closest route. Many organizations start to build a new website without knowing how the old one worked. It's better to start with measuring the existing website and learn from the analysis. The analysis is the base for long-term campaign-based marketing, and is a cost effective way to learn more about your visitors.

## It's All Connected

Traditionally, marketing and advertising have been seen from a pipeline principle. The various types of media were considered as pipelines to invest money for different marketing campaigns. Sometimes the money was placed on tactical, sometimes on strategic advertising. The budget determined the pipeline. If there was money for a TV or cinema advertisement, the choice was simple. Here's a picture of the pipeline principle:

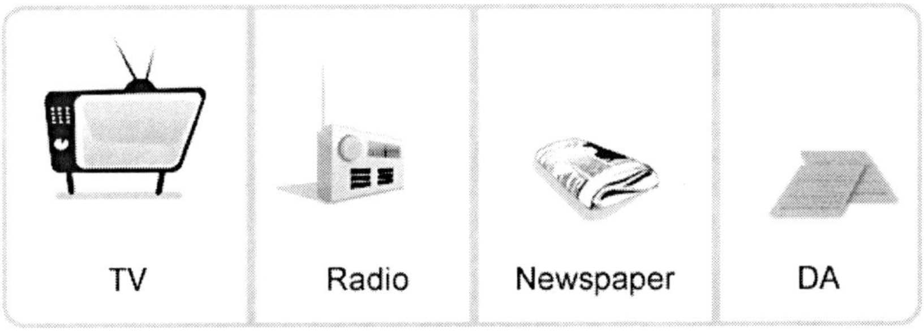


PICTURE 40. Media pipelines

When the Internet came on the scene, it was added as yet another media pipeline, often last in the chain. At the time, advertising agencies didn't realize the new opportunities that the Internet created; they saw it as simply another way to market to a customer. The banner became a common form, since it was something that the advertising branch could compare with their other choices and it was easy to explain to the customer. In the picture below, the Internet has been placed last, which was often caused by lack of funds. The budget was spread across the other pipelines, and if there was something left over, then maybe it could be used for "something fun for the web."

PICTURE 41. Media pipelines with the Internet

Luckily, times have changed, and the possibilities for the Internet and the web have increased. The media pipeline image has also changed in that it's the website that ties all of the marketing together, and in certain cases all communication for a company. Here is a modern picture:

PICTURE 42. A modern picture of the media landscape

Of course, the picture is extremely simplified. There are many other channels for marketing, but the idea is that the Internet surrounds the other media and supports them all in marketing. The pipelines have also started to disappear between the other channels, and marketing is being spread across more media. Somehow, those that have a need end up on the web. With a good web strategy, the possibilities are greater that the visitors will land on the right website and not on a competing page. The work with the strategy starts at the same time that an organization is ready to build a new website. Make sure that there are resources in place that can help make the website profitable and that it will be the marketing punch of the organization. Provide those responsible with all of the functions necessary to create a structured and profitable website.

It's not just advertising that can be linked, but also other types of communication. A simple thing like a press release has many more uses than just having a journalist write about an organization. It can build links, and be optimized for search engines so that it attracts traffic to the website, both directly and indirectly.

There are many people involved in the communication work of a larger organization. There are people who work with the website, there are those who work with campaigns both on and off the web, there are PR people, media purchasers, informants, and others who communicate messages from the organization in some way. When these channels are joined together, there is a need for one person to keep an eye on how all of it connects to the web. A role that will become more common with time is the web controller or communications controller. This is a person who is strategically responsible for an advertisement not sending traffic to a competitor, or making sure that a press release doesn't leave the company without taking search engines into consideration. A web controller can also monitor new services and functions that pop up on the web and make sure that they are exploited by the organization. In the beginning of the web, the technique was so simple that almost anyone could create a website. For example, when the software program PageMaker was launched, everyone could create printed ads – technically. Text and images could be put together quickly to create a brochure. Unfortunately, the appearance and the language left a lot to be desired.

Every new trend and innovation on the web is easy to start up. It's more difficult to manage it in the long run, and to allow it free scope in the organization. The first webs that popped up were made by staff that, in reality, had other tasks. In the beginning, it worked, but it finally became a task that took too much time. In certain cases, management didn't realize the importance of having a website, and the project was put aside because it was deemed too time consuming. The same thing is still happening with the web today. New exciting opportunities arise in a never-ending stream and need to find their place. The web controller will be responsible for monitoring and figuring out how an organization can use these possibilities in the best way, and manage them within the organization's boundaries. Innovations also need to find their place in the overall marketing concept. It's about finding a mix where the web is a part of the marketing plan and is given the space it deserves. A good strategy for using a marketing budget gives the organization the possibility to run structured web work that is measurable and that generates a profit for the organization. That's what I call "Business by web.".

Anders Tufvesson
Karlstad, October 2010

# About TUK Förlag

TUK stands for Training, Education and Knowledge (in Swedish ”Träning, Utbildning och Kunskap” thus the TUK) .

TUK Förlag AB publishes practical leadership literature and has published this book

TUK is run by the owners Tomas Gustavsson and John Johansson. Read more about TUK and what we do at www.tuk.se

CPSIA information can be obtained at www.ICGtesting.com
Printed in the USA
LVOW102113120213

319790LV00029B/1730/P

9 789186 419097